MEDON VERLAG AG   CH-6005 Luzern-St. Niklausen   Villa Unterhasli

Copyright:	© MCMXCI MEDON VERLAG AG, Luzern
Rezepte:	Peter Bührer, Cuisinier, Wallisellen
Fotos:	Michael Wissing, BFF, Freiburg i.Br.
Satz:	TyPOS/Typostutz AG, Rotkreuz
Lithos:	Interrepro AG, Münchenstein
Idee, Gestaltung:	MEDON VERLAG AG, Luzern
ISBN-Nr.	3-906994-06-6

The
New
Swiss
Cuisine

91 recipes
for the modern gourmet

Preface

Swiss chefs are world famous, yet Swiss cuisine is hardly ever mentioned. Thus, the cuisine prepared by Swiss chefs is in fact not genuine Swiss cuisine. It is peculiar that the Swiss cuisine that has been handed down to us has its origins in the poor regions of the country and not in the wealthy cities such as Berne. Evidently the rich patricians had hefty country-women cooking for them, just as the Austrian nobility did. Or else one forbade onself the sensuous pleasure of relishing food, as I believe was the case in puritan Zurich.

Why then does one find an independent cuisine among the folk of the poorer regions rather than among the well-to-do people? Quite likely because more creative thought had to be given to the ingredients – since very few were at hand – in order to bring variety into the menues. What the folk from the Ticino – the poorest of the poor – were able to conjure up from chestnuts never ceases to amaze. The people from the Grisons, cut off from the rest of the world, were full of ideas. The dishes that appear to us well worth copying today were usually only served at feasts – at weddings and at christenings. As we can read in Jeremias Gotthelf's tale «The Black Spider» the long days and nights of slaughtering and cooking were in themselves a feast. Just for this reason, these dishes have an inherent capricious and ornate note that is lacking in everyday «stomach-fillers».

When Peter Bührer – a passionate gastro-archeologist and extraordinarily conscientious master at the stove-rummages in the treasure-chest of Swiss cuisine and serves us a «Bernese Childbed Soup» or a «Prättigau Wedding Pie», only a very few of us might be reminded of traditional home-cooking, familiar dishes and dishes believed lost. He confronts us with meals that are just as innovative as the creations by a Parisian chef. What makes them «Swiss» are merely the traditional and familiar ingredients. A simple grocery store in the countryside, an average butcher's shop and a garden in which the common vegetables and herbs grow, suffice to be able to recreate most of Peter Bührer's recipes. That so much can be created from so little is in my view the great merit of this book.

But that is by no means all. Hard work awaits the cook at home because traditional cuisine can never be a hurried cuisine. It dates back to the period when one took one's time to prepare a meal; when cooking was part of the housewife's moral obligation and was carried out with utmost care and seriousness. The fact that these recipes have been adapted to today's eating habits does not make them easier to prepare – only lighter and more digestible. It may sound somewhat presumptuous to say that an inducement to work is another merit of this book. Far too many cooking instructions have the sole purpose to reduce one's time in the kitchen to a few minutes with the result that nothing gives pleasure – neither the cooking nor the meal.

Can Swiss cuisine still be saved? Probably not even the most patriotic cooks could be enticed to prepare food only in this manner. Far too great are the temptations of Italian, French and even East Asian cuisine. But these lovely dishes created by our forefathers are a welcome alternative at any time and even a small boost to our self-confidence. Without any princely pomp a Swiss cuisine came into being that in spite of its substantialness is a delight for the taste-buds.

Silvio Rizzi

Silvio Rizzi

Silvio Rizzi is an established food critic and publisher of the Swiss Gault-Millau Guide. He is familiar with both gourmet and homestead cuisine, and he attempts to distinguish the genuine from the pretentious.

SPRING

SUMMER

AUTUMN

WINTER

APPENZELLER GITZICHÜECHLI

Goat Fritters with Mushroom Dumplings (Appenzell)

2 carrots
50 g (1.75 oz) knob celery
½ leek
1 onion
1.8 l (8 cups) vegetable bouillon (s. p. 205)
1.2 dl (½ cup) dry white wine
1 twig thyme
1 twig marjoram
2 bay leaves
5 peppercorns, crushed
1 kg (2¼ lbs) goat from the neck

Clean and trim vegetables. Chop coarsely. Pour bouillon and wine into a large kettle. Add herbs and spices. Cut meat into 40 g (1.5 oz) cubes. Add to bouillon. Bring to the boil. Reduce heat and simmer for 1½ hours.

Preparation:
25 minutes
Cooking time:
1 hour 50 minutes
Yields 4 servings

Dumplings:
300 g (10.5 oz) sifted flour
3 eggs
1 Tsp salt
2.5 dl (1 cup) milk
100 g (3.5 oz) spinach, cooked
1 Tb parsley

Place flour in a mixing bowl. Beat eggs. Combine with flour. Gradually stir in milk. Season with salt. Chop spinach and parsely finely. Add to flour mixture. Work into a smooth batter. Fill a large kettle with water. Add salt. Bring to the boil. Rinse a small wooden chopping board with cold water. Spread with 1 Tb batter. Hold board over kettle. With a spatula or a knife cut small strips the size of a small finger and let slide into water. Poach for 8–10 minutes. Remove with a slotted spoon and drain well.

150 g (5.25 oz) chanterelles
40 g (1.5 oz) butter
1 twig thyme

Clean and trim chanterelles. Heat butter in a skillet. Sauté chanterelles. Stir in dumplings and thyme. Sauté until dumplings turn golden. Remove from pan. Keep warm.

Batter:
150 g (5.25 oz) sifted flour
½–1 dl (¼–½ cup) beer
1 Tsp salt
1 egg yolk
20 g (0.75 oz) melted butter
2 egg whites
Flour
Oil for deep-frying

In a mixing bowl combine beer, egg yolks, salt and butter. Work into a smooth batter. Beat egg whites until stiff. Fold into batter. Heat oil. Remove meat from stock and dry with a towel. Dust with flour. Dip into batter. Deep-fry until crisp.

80 g (2.75 oz) butter
1 clove garlic
4–5 rosemary leaves
1 twig tarragon
1 Tb parsley
Salt, freshly ground pepper

Melt butter. Mash garlic. Chop rosemary leaves, tarragon and parsley finely. Add to butter and stir well. Season with salt and pepper. Let butter turn a light brown.

Arrange fritters and dumplings on plates. Sprinkle with butter.

BASLER SALM
Fresh Salmon à la Bâloise

**8 slices of fresh salmon
60 g (2 oz) each, skinned**

**Sauce:
2 small shallots
10 g (0.25 oz) butter
1.5 dl (⅔ cup) dry
white wine
1.5 dl (⅔ cup)bouillon
50 g (1.75 oz) butter
Salt
½ lemon, juice
1 bunch chives**

**Vegetables:
6 large potatoes
10 g (0.25 oz) butter
1 Tsp chervil,
finely chopped**

**400 g (1 lb) mange-tout peas
(snow peas)**

**Salt, freshly ground
white pepper
1 Tb olive oil**

4 large twigs chervil

Remove bones from salmon with a pair of tweezers.

Chop shallots finely. Heat butter in a small saucepan. Sauté shallots. Moisten with wine. Cover with bouillon. Over low heat boil down to ⅓ of its volume. Whisk in butter. Season with salt and a few drops lemon juice. Chop chives finely and add to sauce. Keep warm. Preheat oven to 80°C (176°F).

Peel potatoes and quarter. Cut off hard edges. Fill a kettle with lightly salted water. Boil potatoes until tender. Drain. Keep warm.

Remove ends and strings from snow peas. Wash and drain. Steam or cook «al dente». Keep warm.

Season fish with salt and pepper. Heat oil in a teflon skillet. Sauté fish well on both sides. Set pan in oven for 10 minutes.

Arrange snow peas «fan-like» on plates. Set fish on top. Place potatoes on both sides. Surround fish with sauce. Garnish with chervil.

Preparation:
15 minutes
Cooking time:
20 minutes
Yields 4 servings
as a first course

BERNER CHINDBETTISUPPE
Bernese Childbed Soup (Berne)

2 carrots
1 small knob celery
1 chicken about 1.5 kg (3½ lbs)
2 l (8 cups) chicken bouillon
1 bunch parsley
3 peppercorns, crushed
1 bay leaf

Peel carrots and celery. Chop coarsely. Place in a large kettle. Add chicken. Cover with bouillon. Add parsley and spices. Bring to a boil. Simmer for 50 minutes. Remove chicken from kettle. Bone breast. Cut into strips. Set aside.

1 dl (½ cup) milk
1 dl (½ cup) whipping cream
Salt, freshly ground pepper

Measure 7 dl (3 cups) bouillon and strain through a sieve into a saucepan. Boil down to ⅔ of its volume. Stir in milk and cream. Season with salt and pepper. Set soup aside.

4 small ears corn
Salt

Fill a large kettle with water. Add salt. Cook corn until tender.

½ leek
4 eggs

Trim the leek. Cut into thin slices. Steam until tender. Beat eggs. Bring soup to a boil. Stir in eggs and bring back to the boil.

1 bunch chives

Arrange chicken meat, corn and leeks in soup plates and cover with soup. Cut the chives finely. Sprinkle over soup.

Preparation:
20 minutes
Cooking time:
1 hour 20 minutes
Yields 6 servings

PRÄTTIGAUER HOCHZEITSPASTETE
Prättigau Wedding Pie with Stewed Plums and Salad

420 g (15 oz) veal,
sirloin tip
180 g (6.5 oz) pork, rib cut
220 g (7.75 oz) fresh pork
fat or fat salt pork
1 Tbs salt, freshly ground
pepper
8 leaves sweet basil
1 Tb parsley
40 g (1.5 oz) bread crumbs
1 egg white
0.5 dl (¼ cup)
whipping cream

Terrine to be prepared one day in advance.
Cut meat and pork fat into small cubes (if fat salt pork is used, simmer for 10 minutes to remove salt). Spread on a platter. Season with salt and pepper. Chop herbs. Spread herbs and bread crumbs over meat. Beat egg white lightly. Mix with cream. Pour over meat. Cover with transparent film. Place in refrigerator overnight.

Preparation:
40 minutes
Cooking time:
1 hour 30 minutes
Yields
8–10 servings

1 onion
30 g (1 oz) butter
150 g (5.25 oz) calf's liver
2 Tbs cognac
1.5 dl (⅔ cup) dry
white wine
1 Tsp green pepper,
crushed
1.2 dl (½ cup) whipping
cream
Salt
50 g (1.75 oz) raisins
100 g (3.5 oz) ham, cooked

Heat oven to 140° C (284° F).
Chop onion finely. Heat butter in a skillet. Sauté onions. Add liver and sauté over high heat. Moisten with cognac. Cover with wine. Cut liver into pieces. Season with green pepper. Mix liver with meat. Grind very finely in a food processor. Transfer stuffing to a mixing bowl and place on ice cubes. Season with salt and pepper. Stir in cream. Add raisins. Dice ham and add to stuffing. Blend well. Butter a terrine and fill with mixture. Cover with a lid or aluminium foil. Fill a large roasting pan to ⅔ with water. Place a newspaper on the bottom. Set terrine into pan. Poach for 45–50 minutes. Remove terrine from pan. Let cool.

Salads:
Various salad greens and
water cress

Clean, trim and wash salads. Drain well. Arrange salad on plates.

Vinaigrette:
0.4 dl (¼ cup) raspberry
vinegar
1 dl (½ cup) safflower oil
Salt, freshly ground pepper

Blend all ingredients for the vinaigrette.

16 prunes
1 small shallot
10 g (0.25 oz) butter
0.5 dl (¼ cup) dry
white wine
0.5 dl (¼ cup) water

Wash, pit and quarter prunes. Mince shallot finely. In a skillet heat butter. Sauté shallots. Add prunes. Sauté briefly. Moisten with wine. Bring to the boil and let the liquid reduce somewhat. Season with little salt. Set aside.

Unmold terrine and invert on a platter. Cut into slices.

6 cherry tomatoes

Place terrine next to salad. Surround with prunes. Quarter cherry tomatoes. Garnish plate. Sprinkle salad with vinaigrette.

TAFASER CHRÄPFLI
Meat Turnovers (Davos)

400 g (14 oz) sifted flour
1 egg
1 egg yolk
Salt
Water

Place flour in a mixing bowl. Add salt. Beat egg and egg yolk. Stir into flour. Moisten with water. Work into a smooth dough. Add water if necessary. Let stand for 1 hour.

Preparation:
1 hour
Cooking time:
20 minutes
Yields 4 servings

Filling:
120 g (4.25 oz) slab bacon
1 onion
2 cloves garlic
150 g (5.25 oz) ground beef
30 g (1 oz) butter
1 dl (½ cup) whipping cream

Dice bacon finely. Chop onion finely. Mash garlic. Heat butter in a skillet. Sauté bacon. Add onions, garlic and meat. Sauté briefly. Stir in cream. Blend well. Bring to the boil. Set aside.

100 g (3.5 oz) fresh spinach
10 g (0.25 oz) butter

Wash spinach. Remove stems. Drain well. Heat butter in a casserole. Sauté spinach until wilted. Drain and chop.

2 French rolls, stale
3 egg yolks
Salt, freshly ground pepper

Grate rolls finely. In a mixing bowl blend meat mixture, egg yolks, spinach and bread crumbs. Season with salt and pepper. Blend well. Chill for 1 hour.
Roll out dough as thin as possible. Cut out circles 8 cm (3⅛ inches) in diameter. Place 1 Tb of filling in center. Moisten the edge with water. Fold into semi-circles. Press edges together. Fill a large kettle with water. Add salt. Bring to the boil. Poach turnovers for 5–6 minutes. Remove with a slotted spoon. Keep warm.

1½ Tsp sweet basil
1½ Tsp chervil
1 Tsp marjoram
1½ Tsp parsley
3 cloves garlic
100 g (3.5 oz) butter
Salt, freshly ground pepper

Chop herbs finely. Mash garlic. Heat butter in a small saucepan. Add herbs. Season with salt and pepper. Let butter turn a golden brown. Serve turnovers in soup plates. Spoon with herb butter.

AARGAUER KALBSVORESSEN
Veal Stew with Green Asparagus Tips and Chervil (Aargau)

1 carrot
1 large onion
½ leek
50 g (1.75 oz) knob celery
20 g (0.75 oz) butter
1 dl (½ cup) dry white wine
2 l (8½ cups) vegetable bouillon (s. p. 205)
4 peppercorns
1 bay leaf

Preheat oven to 150° C (302° F).
Clean and trim vegetables. Chop coarsely. Heat butter in a fireproof casserole. Sauté vegetables. Moisten with wine. Cover with bouillon. Add spices. Bring to the boil. Reduce heat and simmer for 20 minutes.

600 g (1½ lbs) veal soulder

Cut the meat into 30 g (1 oz) cubes. Add to bouillon. Set casserole in oven and cook meat for 2 hours.

3 dl (1¼ cups) whipping cream
½ lemon, juice
1 pinch Cayenne pepper
30 g (1 oz) butter

Remove meat with a slotted spoon. Set aside. Strain bouillon through a fine sieve into a saucepan. Stir in cream. Boil down until it thickens slightly. Season with salt and Cayenne. Add a few drops lemon juice. Return meat to sauce. Reheat carefully.

24 green asparagus tips, cooked «al dente»
10 g (0.5 oz) butter

In a skillet heat butter. Add asparagus tips and reheat.

1 bunch chervil

Place stew in center of plates. Surround with asparagus tips. Garnish with chervil.

Preparation:
25 minutes
Cooking time:
2 hours 10 minutes
Yields 4 servings

EMMENTALER LAMMVORESSEN

Lamb Stew (Emmental)

1 carrot
50 g (1.75 oz) knob celery
1 onion
1 bay leaf
1 clove
4 dl (1¾ cups) bouillon

Clean, trim and peel carrot and celery. Stud onion with bay leaf and clove. Pour bouillon into a large kettle. Add vegetables and studded onion. Bring to the boil.

600 g (1¼ lbs) lamb sirloin
30 g (1 oz) butter
1 Tb sifted flour
1 dl (½ cup) dry white wine
1 pinch saffron, ground
1 pinch dried saffron stigmas
2.5 dl (1 cup) whipping cream

Cut meat into 40 g (1.5 oz) cubes. Add to bouillon. Simmer meat for 1½ hours. Remove meat from kettle. Keep warm. Strain bouillon through a fine sieve. Set aside for sauce. Heat butter in a small saucepan. Stir in flour. Moisten with wine. Cover with the bouillon. Add saffron and cream. Bring to the boil. Reduce heat and boil sauce down to 2.5 dl (1 cup). Pour into a blender and mix up briefly. Set aside.

Vegetables:
4 carrots
10 g (0.25 oz) butter
2 dl (⅞ cup) bouillon

Peel carrot and dice. Heat butter in a small saucepan. Turn carrots in the butter. Moisten with bouillon. Add salt. Cook until tender.

3 potatoes
Salt
20 g (0.75 oz) butter

Peel potatoes. Slice and shape into circles. In a kettle bring lightly salted water to the boil. Add potatoes. Boil until tender but crisp. Heat butter in a skillet. Sauté potatoes on both sides until golden brown. Correct seasoning.

Salt, freshly ground pepper
Nutmeg
0.5 dl (¼ cup) whipped cream

Return meat to sauce. Reheat carefully. Season with salt, pepper and nutmeg. Stir in 1 Tb whipped cream.

4 fresh mint leaves

Place meat in center of plates. Surround with carrots and potatoes. Garnish with mint leaves.

Preparation:
20 minutes
Cooking time:
2 hours
Yields 4 servings

24

ENGADINER MAISKNÖDEL
Cornmeal Dumplings with Salads (Engadine)

400 g (14 oz) all-puropse flour
200 g (7 oz) cornmeal
200 g (7 oz) coarse cornmeal
40 g (1.5 oz) dried currants
1 Tsp parsley
20 g (0.75 oz) butter
Salt, freshly ground pepper
1–2 dl (1/2–7/8 cup) milk

In a mixing bowl combine flour and cornmeal. Chop parsley finely and stir in. Add butter and currants. Season with salt and pepper. Gradually stir in milk until batter has a solid texture. Fill a large kettle with water. Add salt. Bring to a boil. Form walnut-size dumplings. Poach for 40–50 minutes.

Various salad greens

Trim, clean and wash salad greens.

Vinaigrette:
1 small shallot
0.6 dl (1/4 cup) herb vinegar
1 Tsp granulated sugar
1.5 dl (2/3 cup) safflower- or sunflower-oil
Salt, freshly ground pepper

Mince shallot and combine with all ingredients for the vinaigrette.

30 g (1 oz) Gruyère, grated
30 g (1 oz) butter

Arrange salad bouquets on plates. Sprinkle with vinaigrette. Transfer dumplings on plates. Sprinkle with cheese. Heat butter until a light brown and spoon over dumplings.

1 large twig parsley

Garnish with parsley.

Preparation:
20 minutes
Cooking time:
1 hour
Yields 6 servings

HACKBRATEN IM NETZ
Meat Loaf in a Caul with Pasta and Apple Sauce

**200 g (7 oz) caul,
ordered from the butcher
½ leek
1 carrot
2 onions
100 g (3.5 oz) mushrooms
½ bunch parsley
2 cloves garlic**

Soak caul in cold water. Chop vegetables, onions, mushrooms and garlic in a cutter.

Preparation:
20 minutes
Cooking time:
1 hour 20 minutes
Yields 4 servings

**30 g (1 oz) butter
2 twigs thyme
Salt**

Heat a teflon skillet. Add butter. Sauté vegetable mixture. Add thyme. Season with salt. Transfer to a mixing bowl. Let cool. Preheat oven to 200°C (390°F). Place empty roasting pan in the oven.

**250 g (8.75 oz) ground beef
250 g (8.75 oz) ground pork
250 g (8.75 oz) uncooked
veal sausage meat
2 eggs
Salt, freshly ground pepper
1 pinch nutmeg
100 g (3.5 oz) bread crumbs**

Add meat to vegetable mixture. Stir in eggs. Blend well. Season with salt and pepper. Blend in bread crumbs. Form into a loaf. Drain caul well. Spread on table. Cut into a 40x50 cm (15¾x19¹⁄₁₆ inches) rectangle. Place loaf in center and wrap thightly.

0.5 dl (¼ cup) cooking-oil

Add oil to hot roasting pan. Sear meat loaf well on all sides. Reduce oven temperature to 160° C (320° F) and roast meat loaf for 1 hour.

**Sauce:
1 onion
10 g (0.25 oz) butter
1 clove garlic
1 twig rosemary
2.5 dl (1 cup) red wine
2.5 dl (1 cup) veal stock
30 g (1 oz) butter
Salt, freshly ground pepper**

Chop onion finely. Heat butter in a saucepan. Sauté onions. Peel and halve garlic. Add to pan. Moisten with wine. Stir in rosemary leaves. Boil mixture down by ⅓. Add veal stock. Boil sauce down by ⅓ more. Whisk in butter. Keep warm.

**Pasta:
1 onion
30 g (1 oz) butter
400 g (14 oz) pasta (lungo-
vermicelli coupe), cooked
40 g (1.5 oz) Gruyère, grated**

Chop onion finely. Heat butter in a skillet. Sauté onions until a light brown. Stir in pasta and heat. Season with salt and pepper. Mix in cheese and stir well. Keep warm.

Apple sauce (s. p. 60)

**Vegetables:
1 knob celery
5 large carrots
25 g (0.75 oz) butter
Salt
1 Tb parsley
1 Tb chervil**

Clean and trim vegetables. Cut into sticks the size of a finger. Cut off sharp edges (turn). Cook «al dente» in lightly salted water. Drain well. Heat butter in a skillet. Sauté vegetables briefly. Chop parsley and chervil finely. Add to vegetables. Correct seasoning. Keep warm.

100 g (3.5 oz) bacon, sliced

Fry bacon until crisp. Slice meat loaf. Place on lower part of plates. Set pasta above meat. Spoon sauce over meat. Garnish with vegetables and bacon.

LAPIN AU MARC
Stewed Rabbit in Marc (Grappa) Sauce (Waadt)

**1 rabbit cut into
serving pieces
Salt, freshly ground pepper
2 Tbs olive oil**

Season rabbit with salt and pepper. Heat oil in a large casserole. Brown meat well on all sides.

**½ leek
1 onion
2 dl (⅞ cup) beef bouillon
3 dl (1¼ cups) veal stock
2 dl (⅞ cup) dry white wine
1 large twig parsley
1 twig marjoram
1 large twig rosemary**

Clean, trim and dice vegetables. Add to meat and stir well. Moisten with wine. Cover with bouillon and veal stock. Add herbs. Cover casserole. Bring to the boil. Reduce heat and simmer meat for 1½ hours.

**Polenta:
5 dl (2⅛ cups) milk
5 dl (2⅛ cups) bouillon
300 g (10.5 oz) cornmeal,
coarse variety
20 g (0.75 oz) butter
20 g (0.75 oz) Gruyère,
grated
100 g (3.5 oz) raisins
Salt, freshly ground pepper**

In a saucepan bring milk and bouillon to the boil. Gradually stir in cornmeal. Mix well. Stirring frequently, cook over low heat for 30–40 minutes. Stir in butter, cheese and raisins. Blend well. Correct seasoning. Keep warm.

**2 leeks
30 g (1 oz) butter**

Clean, trim and wash leeks. Cut lengthwise into strips 2 mm (1/16 inch) in width. Cook in lightly salted water until tender but still crisp. Drain well. Heat butter in a skillet. Sauté leeks briefly. Keep warm.

**1 dl (½ cup) Marc (Grappa)
30 g (1 oz) butter
Salt, freshly ground pepper**

Remove rabbit from casserole. Keep warm. Strain sauce through a fine sieve into another saucepan. Add Marc and bring to the boil. Whisk in butter. Correct seasoning.

Set polenta in the shape of a pedestal in center of serving plates. Place 2 pieces of meat on top. Coat and surround meat with sauce. Garnish with leeks.

Preparation:
20 minutes
Cooking time:
2 hours
Yields 4 servings

LUZERNER OMELETTEN
Omelets with Sweetbreads (Lucerne)

Filling:
500 g (1 lb) sweetbreads

Place the sweetbreads in a bowl. Rinse with running cold water for at least 1 hour.

3 dl (1¼ cups) vegetable bouillon
(s. p. 205)
1 dl (½ cup) dry white wine
Salt

Pour bouillon in a saucepan. Bring to the boil. Add little salt. Place sweetbreads in bouillon and poach for 30 minutes. Let cool. Trim the sweetbreads. Separate into lobs. Remove the filaments of fat, gristle and tubes.

1 small onion
20 g (0.75 oz) butter
Salt, freshly ground pepper
3 Tbs dried currants
1 Tb pine kernels

Chop onion finely. Heat butter in a skillet. Sauté onions. Add sweetbreads and sauté. Season with salt and pepper. Stir in currants and pine kernels. Keep warm.

Omelets:
8 eggs
0.5 dl (¼ cup) milk
Salt
40 g (1.5 oz) butter

In a mixing bowl beat eggs. Stir in milk and mix well. Season with salt. Heat butter in small teflon skillets. Place one quarter of the egg mixture in each pan. Cook omelets until they begin to brown. As soon as the surface begins to settle, spread each omelet with one quarter of the sweetbread mixture. With a spatula lift the edge and roll toward center. Turn omelet over and cook until a light brown.

Sauce:
3 dl (1¼ cups) sour cream
40 g (1.5 oz) Gruyère, grated
Salt, freshly ground pepper

In a small saucepan heat sour cream. Stir in cheese. Season with salt and pepper.
Cook the peas «al dente». Drain.

120 g (4.25 oz) fresh peas
1 large twig parsley

Pour some sauce on each plate. Set omelet in center. Sprinkle with peas. Garnish with parsley.

Preparation:
1 hour
Cooking time:
20 minutes
Yields 4 servings

OBERLÄNDER CHÜNGELIRÜCKEN

Saddle of Rabbit with Ramson Sauce and Salad

2 saddles of rabbit, boned
Salt, freshly ground pepper
2 Tbs cooking-oil

Preheat oven to 120°C (250° F).
Season saddles of rabbit with salt and pepper. Heat oil in a skillet. Sauté saddles on all sides for 2–3 minutes. Transfer to a plate. Place in oven.

Ramson sauce:
4 leaves of ramson
30 g (1 oz) butter
0.5 dl (¼ cup) dry
white wine
2 dl (⅞ cup) veal stock
(s. p. 207)
Salt, freshly ground pepper

Cut the ramson leaves into fine strips. In small saucepan heat very little butter. Sauté ramson strips briefly. Moisten with wine. Cover with veal stock. Over low heat boil down to half its volume. Stir in remaining butter. Correct seasoning. Keep warm.

Salad:
8 green asparagus tips,
cooked
20 g (0.75 oz) dandelion
30 small spinach leaves
2 tomatoes
1 head chicory (endive)
40 g (1.5 oz) salad
various salad greens

Clean, trim and wash salads. Drain well. Skin, seed, juice and dice tomatoes. Arrange salads and tomatoes on plates.

Vinaigrette:
0.4 dl (¼ cup) rasperry
vinegar
1.2 dl (½ cup) safflower oil
Salt, freshly ground pepper
½ Tsp granulated sugar
1 shallot

In a bowl combine all ingredients for the vinaigrette. Mince shallot finely. Add to dressing.

Sprinkle salads with vinaigrette. Cut the saddles of rabbit diagonally into thin slices. Place next to salads. Surround meat with ramson sauce.

Preparation:
10 minutes
Cooking time:
20 minutes
Yields 4 servings

PUSCHLAVER OSTERGITZI
Saddle of Goat with Leek-Risotto

2 saddles of baby goat, boned

Preheat oven to 80°C (176°F).
Have the butcher bone the meat.

2 French rolls, stale
50 g (1.75 oz) almonds, ground
50 g (1.75 oz) raisins
Grated rind of ½ lemon
1 dl (½ cup) milk
2 egg yolks
1 Tsp rosemary leaves
1 large twig marjoram
Salt, freshly ground pepper

Grate French roll finely. In a bowl combine almonds, bread crumbs, raisins and milk. Add lemon rind. Chop rosemary leaves and marjoram finely. Add to mixture. Season with salt and pepper. Blend well. Place saddles on table. Set ½ of the mixture in center of each. Fold and sew or skewer. Season with salt and pepper.

80 g (2.75 oz) butter
2 cloves garlic
1 twig rosemary
Salt, freshly ground pepper

Heat butter in a fireproof casserole. Brown meat well on all sides. Add garlic and rosemary. Set casserole in oven for 1 hour.

2 dl (⅞ cup) dry white wine
1 dl (½ cup) beef bouillon
3 dl (1¼ cups) veal stock (s. p. 207)

Remove meat from casserole. Keep warm. Add wine, bouillon and veal stock to braising juice. Over moderate heat reduce to half its volume.

Leek-Risotto:
3 leeks
30 g (1 oz butter)
300 g (10.5 oz) Italian rice, unpolished
1 dl (½ cup) dry white wine
6 dl (2½ cups) beef bouillon
100 g (3.5 oz) Parmesan cheese, grated
Salt, freshly ground pepper

Clean, trim and wash leeks. Halve lengthwise. Cut into fine strips. Heat butter in a large saucepan. Sauté leeks. Stir in rice and sauté briefly. Moisten with wine. Cover with bouillon. Cook over low heat for 20–25 minutes. Stir in cheese. Correct seasoning.

50 g (1.75 oz) butter

Strain sauce through a fine sieve into a small saucepan. Reheat. Whisk in butter.

1 bunch chervil

Place risotto in center of plates. Slice meat. Set two slices on each plate. Surround with sauce. Garnish with chervil.

Preparation:
30 minutes
Cooking time:
1 hour 20 minutes
Yields 4 servings

SCHAFFHAUSER HECHTKNÖDEL
Pike Quenelles (Schaffhausen)

500 g (1 lb) pike, skinned, boned
1.5 dl (²⁄₃ cup) whipping cream
2 egg whites
2–3 ice cubes, crushed
Salt, freshly ground white pepper
A dash of Pernot
Lemon juice

Cut the pike into small pieces. In a food processor combine fish, cream, egg whites and ice cubes. Process until mixture has a fine texture. Rub through a sieve. Season with salt and pepper. Add a dash of Pernot and a few drops lemon juice. Chill.

Sauce:
1.5 dl (²⁄₃ cup) fish stock (s.p. 206)
1 dl (½ cup) fruity white wine
1.5 dl (²⁄₃ cup) heavy cream
20 g (0.75 oz) butter
Salt, freshly ground pepper
Lemon juice

In a small saucepan combine fish stock and wine. Bring to a boil and reduce to half its volume. Add cream. Bring back to a boil and reduce sauce by ⅓. Whisk in the butter. Season with salt and pepper and a few drops lemon juice. Keep warm.

Vegetables:
1 cucumber
1 large carrot
1 zucchini (courgette)
½ knob celery
10 g (0.25 oz) butter

Peel vegetables and core with a melon baller. Cook separately «al dente». Drain. Heat butter and sauté briefly. Keep warm.

Fish stock:
1 dl (½ cup) dry white wine
1 dl (½ cup) fish stock (s.p. 206)
2 dl (⁷⁄₈ cup) water
Salt

In a saucepan combine wine, fish stock and water. Add salt. Bring to a boil. Remove fish mixture from refrigerator. Dip two tablespoons into hot water and form the quenelles. Poach for 4 minutes.

2 twigs dill

Remove quenelles from pan. Drain well. Arrange 4–5 quenelles on each plate. Surround with sauce. Sprinkle with vegetables. Garnish with dill.

Preparation:
25 minutes
Cooking time:
20 minutes
Yields 4 servings

WOLLISHOFER CHNÖDELSUPPE

Dumpling Soup from Wollishofen

1 onion
1 carrot
½ leek
150 g (5.25 oz) ground beef
2 egg whites
1.2 l (5 cups) meat stock
4 peppercorns
1 bay leaf

Chop onion finely. Chop carrot and leek coarsely. In a bowl blend vegetables, ground meat and egg whites. Transfer to a large saucepan. Cover with bouillon. Add the spices. Place the saucepan on the stove. Bring to the boil. Stir frequently to prevent egg white from sticking to the bottom of the pan. As soon as the boiling point is reached **stop** stirring. Remove pan from heat source and let broth settle for 2 hours. Strain through a cheese cloth or a clean dish cloth.

Dumplings:
1 onion
50 g (1.75 oz) knob celery
1 carrot
1 bunch chervil
30 g (1 oz) butter
100 g (3.5 oz) uncooked
veal sausage meat

Chop onion finely. Mince vegetables. Chop chervil finely. Heat butter in a skillet. Sauté onions. Add vegetables. Sauté briefly. Stir in chervil. Mix well. Let cool. Blend sausage meat and vegetable mixture. Season with little salt and pepper. Bring bouillon to the simmer. Form dumplings with two teaspoons. Poach for 10 minutes.

1 small zucchini (courgette)
1 carrot
12 green asparagus tips,
cooked

Slice zucchini and carrot lengthwise. Cut into fancy shapes with a tiny cookie-cutter. In a saucepan bring water to the boil. Cook decorations «al dente». Stir asparagus tips and vegetables into soup.

Preparation:
30 minutes
Cooking time:
2 hours 20 minutes
Yields 4 servings

ZÜRI-GSCHNÄTZLETS
Scalopped Veal à la Zurichoise (Zurich)

600 g (1½ lbs) potatoes
Salt, freshly ground pepper
50 g (1.75 oz) leek
50 g (1.75 oz) diced bacon
20 g (0.75 oz) butter

Boil the potatoes at least 1–2 days in advance. Peel potatoes and grate. Season with salt and pepper. Slice leek finely. Heat butter in a skillet. Combine potatoes, bacon and leeks in the pan. Mix well. Form a cake. Sauté until there is a golden brown crust. Turn and sauté other side until golden brown.

400 g (1 lb) tender veal,
sliced into fine strips
20 g (0.75 oz) butter

Heat butter in a skillet. Sear meat well on all sides. Remove from pan. Keep warm.

150 g (5.5 oz) veal kidney,
trimmed
Salt, freshly ground pepper

Slice kidney. Season with salt and pepper. Sear briefly on both sides. Keep warm.

1 small shallot
150 g (5.5 oz) fresh
mushrooms
20 g (0.75 oz) butter
1 dl (½ cup) dry white wine
1 dl (½ cup) whipping cream
1 dl (½ cup) veal stock
(s. p. 207)

Chop shallot finely. Clean, trim and slice mushrooms. Heat butter. Sauté shallots. Add mushrooms and sauté briefly. Moisten with wine and let liquid evaporate. Cover with cream and veal stock. Cook sauce until it reaches a creamy consistency.

1 Tsp parsley
3 Tbs whipped cream

Chop parsely finely. Place meat in sauce. Reheat carefully. Correct seasoning. Stir in parsley. Fold in whipped cream.

Arrange potatoes and meat on plates. Place the kidney in the sauce and serve.

Preparation:
25 minutes
Cooking time:
45 minutes
Yields 4 servings

BERNER OSTERKUCHEN
Bernese Easter Cake with Strawberry Sauce

125 g (4.5 oz) rice, unpolished
Little salt

Fill a saucepan with water. Bring to the boil. Add a pinch of salt. Stir in rice. Cook until tender. Drain.

7.5 dl (3¼ cups) milk
60 g (2.25 oz) butter

Bring milk to the boil. Stir in rice and butter. Cook rice to a pudding-like consistency. Let cool somewhat.

125 g (4.5 oz) almonds, ground
1 lemon
120 g (4.25 oz) granulated sugar
60 g (2.25 oz) dried raisins
60 g (2.25 oz) dried currants
4 egg yolks
4 egg whites
1 pinch salt
kirsch

Peel the lemon. Cut rind into very thin strips (julienne). Blend sugar, almonds, currants and lemon rind with rice. Add egg yolks while stirring continuously. Add a dash of kirsch. Let cool. Add a pinch of salt to egg whites. Beat until stiff. Fold into rice mixture.

150 g puff pastry
Butter for the flan ring
Flour
Confectioner's sugar

Heat oven to 180°C (356°F).
Butter a flan ring 26 cm (10½ inches) in diameter. Dust with flour.
Roll out the puff pastry to a thickness of 3 mm (⅛ inch). Line the flan ring. Prick with a fork. Spread the rice mixture evenly. Bake for 50–60 minutes. Let cool. Dust generously with confectioner's sugar.

Strawberry sauce:
200 g (7 oz) strawberries
2 Tbs water
20 g (0.75 oz) confectioner's sugar
2 Tbs kirsch

Wash and hull the strawberries. Place in a blender. Add 2 Tbs water. Purée. Rub through a fine sieve. Stir in confectioner's sugar and kirsch.

Coat one part of plate with strawberry sauce. Set a piece of cake on the other part.

The easter cake can be prepared in small individual flan rings. Baking time 20 minutes.

Preparation:
25 minutes
Cooking time:
1 hour 30 minutes
Yields 4 servings

FRAISES DU VALAIS
Strawberries in Pinot Noir Cream

Vanilla ice-cream:
1.5 dl (²/₃ cup) milk
3.5 dl (1½ cups) whipping cream
1 vanilla bean, slit open
150 g (5.25 oz) granulated sugar
4 egg yolks

In a saucepan combine milk, cream and vanilla bean. Bring to a boil. Beat egg yolks and sugar until light and lemon-colored. Gradually stir in the hot liquid. Strain through a fine sieve and return to saucepan. Over low heat beat until cream thickens. Let cool. Freeze.

Preparation: :
25 minutes
Cooking time:
30 minutes
Yields 4 servings

Pinot noir cream:
7 dl (3 cups) Pinot noir wine
1 stick cinnamon
2 black peppercorns, crushed
4 Tbs granulated sugar
2 dl (⁷/₈ cup) heavy cream

In a saucepan combine wine, sugar and spices. Bring to a boil and reduce to ⅓ of its volume. Strain syrup through a fine sieve. Let cool. Fold in heavy cream. Set aside.

500 g (1 lb) strawberries
1 lemon, juice
2 Tbs confectioner's sugar
1 Tsp vanilla sugar

Wash and hull strawberries. Slice finely. Dust with confectioner's sugar and vanilla sugar. Sprinkle with lemon juice. Let stand for 1 hour.
Arrange the strawberries in two circles with tips facing outward. Set the ice-cream in center. Surround strawberries with Pinot noir cream and spoon some cream over the ice-cream.

46

RHABARBERTORTE
Tart of Rhubarb with Strawberries and Cinnamon Ice-Cream

Cinnamon ice-cream:
2 dl (⅞ cup) milk
2 dl (⅞ cup) cream
4 egg yolks
80 g (2.75 oz) granulated sugar
3 Tbs ground cinnamon

In a saucepan bring milk and cream to a boil. Beat egg yolks and sugar until light and lemon-colored. Blend in cinnamon. Gradually stir hot liquid into egg mixture. Return to saucepan. Over low heat beat until it thickens. Let cool. Freeze.

Pastry dough:
80 g (2.75 oz) butter
100 g (3.5 oz) granulated sugar
1 egg
1 pinch salt
½ vanilla bean, scraped
0.4 dl (¼ cup) whipping cream
Grated rind of ½ lemon
150 g (5.25 oz) sifted flour
100 g (3.5 oz) almonds, ground

In a mixing bowl beat butter and sugar until smooth and creamy. Beat egg and add salt. Stir into mixture. Add vanilla seeds, cream and grated lemon rind. Stir in flour and almonds. Rapidly work into a smooth solid dough. Cover and chill for 1 hour.

Rhubarb:
400 g (1 lb) rhubarb
50 g (1.75 oz) granulated sugar
0.5 dl (¼ cup) water

Wash, trim and skin rhubarb. Cut diagonally into slices. Spread the bottom of a flat pan with sugar and place rhubarb on top. Add water. Bring to a quick boil. Remove pan from heat. Let rhubarb cool.

2 dl (⅞ cup) heavy cream
2 Tbs kirsch
1 vanilla bean, slit
4 egg yolks

Remove rhubarb from liquid with a slotted spoon. Transfer to a bowl. Stir in cream, kirsch, egg yolks and sugar. Add vanilla seeds. Blend well.
Heat oven to 180°C (356°F).

Butter for the flan ring
Flour for dusting
3 Tbs coarse sugar

Butter a flan ring (26 cm [10¼ inches] in diameter). Dust with flour. Roll out pastry dough to a thickness of 3 mm (⅛ inch) and line flan ring. Form a rim around the edge. Prick with a fork. Line with aluminium foil. Fill with dry beans. Bake blind for 10 minutes. Remove beans and foil. Spread bottom with rhubarb mixture. Set in oven and bake for 15–20 minutes. Sprinkle with coarse sugar. Continue baking for 10 minutes.

Strawberry sauce:
400 g (1 lb) strawberries
100 g (3.5 oz) granulated sugar
0.5 dl (¼ cup) water
2 Tbs kirsch

Wash and hull strawberries. Place in a saucepan. Add sugar, kirsch and water. Bring to the boil. Purée in a blender. Rub through a fine sieve. Set aside.

Confectioner's sugar
2 Tbs pistachio nuts, peeled

Cut the tart into six pieces. Transfer on plates. Spoon some strawberry sauce on one side. Scoop ice-cream and set on sauce. Dust with confectioner's sugar. Chop pistachio nuts. Garnish plate.

Preparation:
15 minutes
Cooking time:
35–40 minutes
Yields 6 servings

SEELÄNDER WALDMEISTERMOUSSE
Woodruff Mousse with Strawberries

4 sheets gelatin

2 egg yolks
75 g (2.5 oz) granulated sugar
2.5 dl (1 cup) milk
20 g (0.75 oz) woodruff
2.5 dl (1 cup) whipping cream

300 g (10.5 oz) strawberries
Juice of ½ lemon
2 Tbs confectioner's sugar

3 Tbs heavy cream
6 fresh mint leaves
Confectioner's sugar

Soak gelatin in little water.

In a mixing bowl beat eggs and sugar until light and lemon-colored. In a saucepan bring milk to a boil. Drain gelatin and add to milk. Stir until it has dissolved. Gradually beat the hot liquid into egg mixture. Stir until cool. Remove stems from woodruff and chop flowers and leaves finely. Beat cream until stiff. Stir woodruff and cream into mousse mixture. Turn custard into 6 prepared molds. Chill for about 6 hours.

Wash and hull strawberries. Purée in a blender and rub through a sieve. Stir in confectioner's sugar and lemon juice.

Unmold mousse and turn on dessert plates. Surround with sauce. Decorate the sauce with heavy cream. Garnish with mint leaves and dust with confectioner's sugar.

Preparation:
15 minutes
Cooking time:
10 minutes
Yields 6 servings

KREBSE VOM MAUENSEE
Crayfish in Liquid

½ **leek** ½ **stalk celery** ½ **bulb fennel** **2 carrots**	Wash, clean and trim the vegetables. Slice very finely. Fill a saucepan with cold water. Add salt. Cook all the vegetables «al dente». Rinse under running cold water. Set aside.
5 medium-sized potatoes	Peel potatoes. Quarter and cut the edges off. Boil until tender. Keep warm.
About 30 large crayfish	Fill a large kettle with water. Add salt. Bring to a boil. Plunge the crayfish into the boiling water. Blanch for 1 minute. Cool immediately in ice-water. Remove the heads. Take the tails out of the shells. Remove intestins. Set aside.
3 dl (1¼ cups) fish stock (s. p. 206) **1 dl (½ cup) dry white wine** **30 g (1 oz) butter** **Salt, freshly ground pepper** **Juice of ½ lemon**	In a saucepan bring fish stock and wine to a boil and reduce to half its volume. Whisk in the butter. Season with salt, pepper and a few drops of lemon juice. Add the crayfish, vegetables and potatoes. Reheat carefully.
1 large twig dill **1 large twig chervil**	Serve in soup bowls and garnish with dill and chervil.

Preparation:
20 minutes
Cooking time:
25 minutes
Yields 4 servings

KUTTELSALAT
Salad of Tripe with Radishes and Tomatoes

250 g (8.75 oz) veal tripe
1 l (4¼ cups) meat bouillon
1 Tb vinegar of Modena
2 Tbs safflower oil or
sunflower oil

Cut the tripe into fine strips. In a kettle bring the bouillon to a boil. Add the tripe and cook for 1 hour 10 minutes. Drain well. Transfer to a bowl. Marinate with vinegar and oil.

Preparation:
20 minutes
Cooking time:
approx. 1 hour
Yields 4 servings

300 g (10.5 oz) various
salad greens

Clean, trim and wash the salad greens.

1 Tb vinegar of Modena
4 Tbs safflower oil
Salt, freshly ground pepper
8 cherry tomatoes
3 red radishes

Mix all the ingredients for the vinaigrette. Quarter the cherry tomatoes. Slice the radishes finely.

1 small shallot
1 bunch chives

On each plate arrange a bouquet with salad greens. Place the tripe in between the leaves. Garnish with tomatoes and radishes. Sprinkle with vinaigrette. Garnish with finely chopped chives and minced shallots.

OCHSENMAULSALAT
Salad of Pressed Ox Muzzle

400 g (14 oz) pressed ox muzzle

Have the pressed ox muzzle finely sliced by the butcher.

1 head chicory (endive)
200 g (7 oz) various salad greens

Clean, trim and wash salads.

0.7 dl (⅓ cup) herb vinegar
0.5 (¼ cup) beef stock
1.5 dl (⅔ cup) safflower oil
Salt, freshly ground pepper
1 shallot
2 tomatoes
1 Tsp fresh chervil

In a bowl blend vinegar, bouillon and oil. Season with salt and pepper. Chop chervil and shallot finely. Skin, peel, seed and dice tomatoes. Blend shallot, chervil and tomatoes with vinaigrette.

2 slices toast
10 g (0.25 oz) butter
1 shallot
8 cherry tomatoes
3 red radishes

Remove rind from bread. Cut slices into small cubes. Heat butter and sauté until crisp. Slice shallot finely. Quarter cherry tomatoes. Slice radishes finely.

Arrange ox muzzle and salads on plates. Sprinkle with vinaigrette. Garnish with croûtons, radishes, shallots and tomatoes.

Preparation:
10 minutes
Cooking time:
15 minutes
Yields 4 servings

ÄLPLERMAGRONEN
The Alpine Farmer's Macaroni with Applesauce

200 g (7 oz) potatoes

3 onions
40 g (1.5 oz) butter
½ clove garlic, mashed
3 dl (1¼ cups) whipping cream
400 g (15 oz) macaroni, cooked
Salt, freshly ground pepper
40 g Gruyère
20 g Fribourg Vacherin

Apple sauce:
1 kg cooking apples
120 g (4.25 oz) granulated sugar
1 stick cinnamon
1 clove
¼ vanilla bean, slit open
1 dl (½ cup) water
Lemon juice (optional)

Boil the potatoes in their skin. Let cool.

Peel onions and cut into thin slices. In a large frying-pan heat the butter and sauté onions until a light brown. Moisten with cream. Add the garlic. Bring to a boil. Stir in the macaroni. Slice the potatoes and stir into pan. Reheat. Grate the cheese and stir in.

Peel and core apples. Cut into small pieces. In a saucepan bring water and sugar to a boil. Add the apples and the spices. Cook until tender. Remove the spices. Purée apples in a blender. Return to saucepan. Bring to a simmer and let the liquid evaporate some-what. Correct seasoning with a few drops lemon juice and sugar if necessary. Place macaroni-potatoe mixture and the apple sauce on plates.

Preparation:
40 minutes
Cooking time:
30 minutes
Yields 4 servings

APPENZELLER CHRUTCHRÄPFLI
Swiss Chard and Spinach Turnovers (Appenzell)

**300 g (10.5 oz) leaves
of Swiss chard
200 g (7 oz) fresh spinach
1 large onion
20 g (0.75 oz) butter
2 dl (7/8 cup) whipping
cream
2 Tbs pine kernels
100 g (3.5 oz) raisins
4 Tbs Gruyère, grated
Salt, freshly ground pepper**

Wash Swiss chard and separate leaves from shoots. Remove stems from spinach. Chop all leaves coarsely. Chop onion finely. Heat butter in a large casserole. Sauté onions. Add chard and spinach. Sauté briefly. Stir in cream. Bring to the boil. Add pine kernels, raisins and cheese. Cook for about 5 minutes or until sauce thickens. Season with salt and pepper. Let cool.

**200 g puff pastry
1 egg white
1 egg yolk**

Preheat oven to 200°C (396°F).
Roll out puff pastry to a thickness of 2 mm (1/16 inch). Cut out circles 8 cm (3 1/8 inches) in diameter. Place 1–2 Tbs vegetable mixture in center. Brush edge with egg white. Fold into semicircles. Press edges together. Place turnovers on a buttered baking sheet. Brush with egg yolk. Bake for 5–7 minutes, or, until a golden brown.

**Sauce:
1 onion
20 g (0.75 oz) butter
2 dl (7/8 cup) whipping
cream
1 dl (1/2 cup) heavy cream
1 Tb Gruyère, grated
1 Tb chervil, finely chopped
1 tomato, skinned, seeded,
juiced, diced**

Chop onion finely. Heat butter in a small saucepan. Sauté onions. Stir in cream and heavy cream. Add cheese, chervil and tomatoes. Stir well. Boil until sauce reaches a creamy consistency. Season with salt and pepper.

Fresh herbs for garnishing

Coat plates with sauce. Set turnovers in center. Garnish with fresh herbs.

Preparation:
20 minutes
Cooking time:
30 minutes
Yields 4 servings

BASLER LUMMELIBRATEN
Fillet of Beef with Potato Dumplings (Basle)

Dumplings:
500 g (1 lb) potatoes
2 egg yolks
30 g (1 oz) bread crumbs
Salt, freshly ground pepper
1 pinch nutmeg
30 g (1 oz) butter

Preheat oven to 90°C (194°F).
Peel potatoes. Grate, wrap into clean towel and drain water. Transfer to a bowl. Mix with egg yolks and bread crumbs. Season with salt, pepper and nutmeg. Blend well. Fill a large kettle with cold water. Add salt. Bring to a boil. Form balls the size of a walnut with the potato mixture. Poach dumplings for 10 minutes. Remove from kettle and drain well. Heat butter in a skillet and sauté dumplings until golden brown. Keep warm.

Fillet of beef:
1 small onion
1 Tb parsely
1 Tb chervil
½ clove garlic
Salt, freshly ground pepper
150 g (5.5 oz) strips fresh pork fat
(4 mm [³/₁₆ inch]) in width
500 g (1 lb) fillet of beef
4 Tbs cooking-oil

Chop onion and herbs finely. Mash garlic. Transfer to a bowl. Season with salt and pepper. Marinate the pork strips for 20 minutes. Lard the beef all around its edge. Heat oil and sear the meat well on all sides for 5–6 minutes. Then place in oven for 25 minutes. (As alternative to fresh pork fat, use fat salt pork and simmer in water for 10 minutes.)

Sauce:
½ leek
1 small onion
200 g (7 oz) chanterelles
20 g (0.75 oz) butter
0.5 dl (¼ cup) dry white wine
2 dl (⅞ cup) whipping cream
1 dl (½ cup) heavy cream
1 bunch chives

Chop leek and onion finely. Clean, trim and halve chanterelles. Heat butter in a skillet. Sauté leeks and onions. Add chanterelles and sauté briefly. Moisten with wine. Add cream and heavy cream. Bring to the simmer and cook sauce for 3–4 minutes. Season with salt and pepper. Chop chives finely and stir into sauce.

1 bunch chervil

Slice the meat into serving portions. Drain the juice. Place on lower part of the plate. Pour the sauce on upper part of plate and set dumplings on sauce. Garnish with chervil.

Preparation:
1 hour
Cooking time:
1 hour
Yields 4 servings

64

BUCHWEIZEN-PIZOKEL

Buckwheat Dumplings

150 g (5.25 oz) buckwheat flour
150 g (5.25 oz) sifted flour
2 eggs
2 dl (⅞ cup) milk
Salt, freshly ground pepper
Nutmeg

Place flour in a mixing bowl. Beat eggs. Add to flour. Gradually blend milk with flour. Work into a smooth creamy batter. Season with salt and pepper.
Fill a large kettle with water. Add salt. Bring to the boil. Rinse a small chopping board with cold water. Spread 2 Tbs batter onto board. Hold over kettle. With a spatula or a knife cut small strips and let slide into water. Poach for 3–4 minutes. Remove with a slotted spoon. Keep warm.

Preparation:
10 minutes
Cooking time:
20 minutes
Yields 4 servings

BUSECCA TICINESE
Tripe Soup with Garlic Bread (Ticino)

3 Tbs Borlotti beans

Soak beans overnight.
Drain beans. Cook in lightly salted water until tender. Drain. Set aside.

3 carrots
1 leek
1 small knob celery

Clean, trim and wash the vegetables. Use a canelle knife for fluting carrots. Then slice finely. Slice the leek diagonally. Slice the celery finely and cut into squares.

500 g (1 lb) honeycomb tripe

Cut the tripe into strips 4 cm (1⁹⁄₁₆ inches) long and 2 mm (¹⁄₁₆ inch) wide. Fill a kettle with water. Add salt. Bring to the boil. Add tripe and cook for 2½ hours. Drain.

30 g (1 oz) butter
1 clove garlic, mashed
1 Tb tomato paste
1.2 l (5 cups) bouillon
¼ Tsp caraway seeds
1 twig thyme
Salt, freshly ground pepper
80 g (2.75 oz) Parmesan, grated
1 twig parsley

In a saucepan heat butter. Sauté vegetables briefly. Add tripe, garlic and tomato paste. Sauté briefly. Moisten with bouillon. Simmer for 20 minutes. Season with caraway, thyme, salt and pepper. Add Borlotti beans and heat.
Serve in soup plates. Sprinkle with cheese or serve separately. Garnish soup with parsley.

Garlic bread:
200 g (7 oz) French bread
50 g (1.75 oz) butter
4 cloves garlic, mashed
10 g (0.25 oz) Gruyère, grated
1 Tb parsley
Salt, freshly ground black pepper

Cut bread into thin slices. Toast in oven. Beat butter until creamy. Chop parsley finely. Blend butter with garlic, cheese and parsley. Season with salt and pepper. Spread bread with butter mixture. Gratinate under broiler until golden brown. Serve with soup.

Preparation:
20 minutes
Cooking time:
3 hours
Yields 6 servings
as a first course.
As a main course
double the ingredients

FORELLENFILET NACH ZUGERART

Filet of Trout à la Zougoise

8 filets of trout

1 small shallot
20 g (0.75 oz) butter
0.4 dl (¼ cup) dry
white wine
1 dl (½ cup) fish stock
(s. p. 206)
1 dl (½ cup) whipping
cream
0.5 dl (¼ cup) heavy cream
1 Tsp parsley
1 Tsp chervil
1 Tsp tarragon
Salt, freshly ground
white pepper
A few drops lemon juice

8 baby carrots
4 baby leeks
4 scallions (spring onions)
20 g (0.75 oz) butter

Garnishings:
Chervil
Tarragon
1 lemon

Skin the trout fillets and bone with a pair of tweezers.

Peel shallot and chop finely. In a skillet heat the butter. Sauté shallots. Place the fish in the pan. Moisten with fish stock and wine. Poach briefly over low heat. Remove fish from pan. Cover and keep warm. Add cream and heavy cream to liquid. Chop the herbs finely and stir into sauce. Simmer until sauce reaches a creamy consistency. Season with salt, pepper and lemon juice.

Steam the vegetables. Heat the butter and sauté.

Place the trout fillets on plates. Nap with sauce. Decorate with vegetables. Garnish with herbs and lemon slices.

Preparation:
15 minutes
Cooking time:
25 minutes
Yields 4 servings

GEDÄMPFTER SCHINKEN
Ham Braised in Hallauer Wine with Potato Salad

1 ham, cured
5 dl (2⅛ cup) Hallauer wine
(a light red wine)
1 onion, diced
2 carrots, diced
10 peppercorns, crushed
1 bay leaf
4 juniper berries

In a large kettle combine ham, wine, vegetables and spices. Bring to the boil. Reduce heat and simmer ham for 1½ hours. Ham can be served either warm or cold.

Preparation:
20 minutes
Cooking time:
1 hour 30 minutes
Yields 4 servings

Potato Salad:
600 g (1¼ lbs) potatoes

Boil potatoes in their skin. Peel. Cut into 3–5 mm (⅛–³⁄₁₆ inch) slices. Transfer to a bowl.

1 onion, finely chopped
1 leek, cut into thin strips
100 g (3.5 oz) bacon,
cut into strips
10 g (0.25 oz) butter
1 Tsp mustard
3–5 dl (1¼–2⅛ cup) bouillon
Salt, freshly ground pepper
0.5 dl (¼ cup) herb vinegar
½ bunch chives,
finely chopped

In a skillet heat butter. Sauté leeks and bacon. Stir in mustard. Moisten with bouillon. Bring to the boil. Pour over potatoes. Add vinegar and chives. Blend carefully. Correct seasoning.

½ bunch fresh chervil

Slice ham into serving pieces. Arrange on plates with potato salad. Garnish with chervil.

GEFÜLLTE KALBSBRUST
Stuffed Breast of Veal with Onion-Potatoes

1.5 kg (3¼ lbs) breast of veal, boned

Stuffing:
2 carrots
50 g (1.25 oz) knob celery
½ leek
1 clove garlic
3 marrow bones
30 g (1 oz) butter
100 g (3.5 oz) calf's brains, trimmed, poached, chopped
70 g (2.5 oz) Gruyère, grated
2 eggs
Salt, freshly ground pepper
Nutmeg
80 g (2.75 oz) ham, cooked

1 onion
Salt, freshly ground pepper
2 Tbs clarified butter
3 dl (1¼ cups) dry white wine
3 dl (1¼ cups) bouillon
1 twig thyme

2 dl (⅞ cup) veal stock (s. p. 207)
50 g (1.75 oz) butter, chilled
Salt, freshly ground pepper

600 g (1¼ lbs) potatoes
Salt
20 g (0.75 oz) clarified butter

2 onions
20 g (0.75 oz) clarified butter

Cut the breast into a square. Sew on two sides to make a pocket.

Clean, trim and dice carrots and celery. Slice leek finely. Mince garlic. Remove marrow from bone and chop. In a skillet heat butter. Sauté vegetables and marrow. Let cool. Stir in brain, cheese and eggs. Season with salt, pepper and nutmeg. Slice ham into small sticks. Spread half the mixture into meat pocket, making an even layer. Top with ham. Cover with remaining stuffing. Skewer or sew to close. Preheat oven to 150°C (302°F).

Chop onion finely. Season veal breast with salt and pepper. Heat oil in a roasting pan. Brown meat well on all sides. Add onions and sauté briefly. Add thyme. Moisten with wine and cover with bouillon. Set pan in oven and braise uncovered for 2 hours. Baste meat frequently with juice.

Remove meat from pan. Keep warm. Strain the sauce through a fine sieve into a small saucepan. Add veal stock. Boil down to half its volume. Whisk in the butter. Correct seasoning. Keep warm.

Peel potatoes and slice finely. Blanch in salted boiling water for 2 minutes. Drain well. Heat clarified butter in a skillet. Sauté potatoes until golden brown. Correct seasoning.

Peel onions. Slice finely. Heat clarified butter and sauté onions well.

Slice the meat into serving portion. Arrange on plates. Spoon sauce around meat. Place potatoes on the side. Garnish with sautéed onions.

Preparation:
30 minutes
Cooking time:
2 hours
Yields 8 servings

GLARNER CHALBERWÜRSCHTLI
Small Veal Sausages with Mashed Potatoes, Pears and Prunes (Glarus)

12 prunes

Soak the prunes one day in advance.

1 kg (2 lbs) potatoes
3 onions
50 g (1.75 oz) butter
8 small veal sausages
2 dl (⅞ cup) meat bouillon
2 dl (⅞ cup) whipping cream

Peel potatoes, quarter and boil until tender. Peel onions and slice finely. Heat butter. Sauté onions without letting them brown. Place the sausages in the pan. Cover with cream and bouillon. Simmer for 15–20 minutes.

1 ripe unblemished pear
30 g (1 oz) granulated sugar
0.4 dl (¼ cup) water
Salt, nutmeg

Peel and core the pear. Slice finely. Caramelize the sugar in a small saucepan. Add the pears and turn. Moisten with wine. Let the sugar dissolve. Set aside.

Remove sausages from pan. Cover and keep warm. Over moderate heat boil the sauce down by one third. Purée in a blender. Season with salt, pepper and nutmeg. Keep warm.

2 dl (⅞ cup) whipping cream
100 g (3.5 oz) butter
Salt, nutmeg

Pass the potatoes through the food mill. Whip in the butter and cream. Season with salt and nutmeg.

150 g (5.25 oz) fresh spinach
30 g (1 oz) butter

Chop the spinach coarsely. Heat butter in a small pan. Sauté the spinach briefly. Season with salt and nutmeg.

1 Tb whipped cream

Heat the prunes in their soaking water. Stir the pears into mashed potatoes. Reheat the sauce. Stir in 1 Tb whipped cream.

2 medium-sized onions
2 Tbs sifted flour
Oil for frying

Slice onions finely. Dust with flour. Heat the oil and deep-fry until crisp.

Place mashed potatoes in the center of plates. Lay the spinach beside and place sausages on top. Nap with sauce. Garnish with prunes and fried onions.

Preparation:
20 minutes
Cooking time:
1 hour 20 minutes
Yields 4 servings

GSOTTNIGS OCHSENFLEISCH
Boiled Beef with Vegetables and Apple-Horseradish Sauce

200 g (7 oz) fresh pork fat, cut into sheets
2 Tbs parsley
1 onion
1 clove garlic
2 Tbs vegetable oil
1 Tsp salt

Chop parsley, onion and garlic finely. Blend with oil. Season with salt. Marinate pork fat for 30 minutes. (As alternative to fresh pork fat, use fat salt pork and simmer for 10 minutes to remove salt.)

Preparation:
50 minutes
Cooking time:
3 hours
Yields 4 servings

750 g (⅔ lbs) beef (London broil, flank)

Bard the meat. Tie with string.

3 l (12¾ cups) beef bouillon

In a large kettle bring bouillon to the boil. Add meat. Cover kettle. Simmer meat for 2½ hours.

Vegetables:
8 baby carrots
1 savoy cabbage
8 baby green kohlrabi
4 large potatoes

Clean, trim and wash vegetables. Quarter cabbage. Steam until tender but still crisp. Remove stalk from cabbage after having steamed it. Peel potatoes. Boil in lightly salted water until tender.

Apple-Horseradish sauce:
4–5 Tbs fresh horseradish
2 apples
1 dl (½ cup) whipping cream
Salt
1 Tsp lemon juice

Grate horseradish finely. Peel apples and grate finely. Mix apples and horseradish. Whip cream until stiff. Blend with apples and horseradish. Season with salt and a few drops lemon juice.

Vinaigrette:
3 tomatoes
1 dl (½ cup) grape seed oil
0.5 dl (¼ cup) herb vinegar
0.5 dl (¼ cup) bouillon
Salt, freshly ground pepper
1 Tb chervil, finely chopped

Skin, seed, juice and dice tomatoes. Blend with all ingredients for vinaigrette.

Slice meat into serving pieces. Arrange meat, vegetables and potatoes on plates. Sprinkle vegetables with vinaigrette. Decorate with apple-horseradish sauce. Serve remaining sauce in a sauce boat.

GESALZENE SCHWEINSBÄCKLI

Lentil Salad with Salted Pork

36 g (1.25 oz) salt
8 g (0.25 oz) sugar
600 g (1½ lbs) pork shank

Blend salt and sugar. Rub pork well on all sides. Place in a bowl. Cover and marinate for 5 days in the refrigerator. Turn over daily and repeat seasoning with the salt/sugar mixture.

1 onion
1 bay leaf
1 clover

Peel onion. Fill a large kettle with cold water. Add salt. Place meat, onion and spices in the kettle. Bring to a simmer and cook meat for 25–30 minutes. Let meat cool in the stock. Keep lukewarm.

Lentil salad:
100 g (3.5 oz) orange lentils
1 twig thyme
1 l (4¼ cups) vegetable bouillon (s. p. 205)

Bring the vegetable bouillon to the boil. Add the lentils and the thyme. Simmer over low heat for about 35 minutes. Strain and set lentils aside.

Mayonnaise:
2 egg yolks
¼ Tsp mustard
1.5 dl (⅔ cup) safflour oil
Lemon juice
Water
Salt, freshly ground white pepper

Blend egg yolks and mustard. Beat until thick and lemon-colored. With a wire-whisk beat in the oil. Drop by drop at first increasing the amount as the mayonnaise thickens. Thin with little water. Season with lemon juice, salt and pepper.

Vinaigrette:
3 Tbs raspberry vinegar
2 Tbs herb vinegar
0.6 dl (¼ cup) safflower oil
0.4 dl walnut oil
1 Tsp parsley, finely chopped

In a bowl blend all the ingredients for the vinaigrette.

1 head chicory (endive) and various salad greens
2 large twigs chervil

Clean, trim and wash the salad greens. Cut the meat into slices.

Arrange a salad bouquet on the plate. Place lentils beside the salad in the shape of a broad stripe. Set meat on top. Sprinkle salad and lentils with vinaigrette. Fill the mayonnaise into a pastry bag and decorate dish. Garnish with chervil.

Preparation:
20 minutes
Cooking time:
1 hour
Marinating:
5 days
Yields 4 servings

SAFTPLÄTZLI
Casserole of Beef with Potato Patties

8 slices beef (top round)
60 g (2 oz) each
Salt, freshly ground pepper
15 g (0.5 oz) sifted flour
2 Tbs cooking-oil

Preheat oven to 180°C (356°F).
Season meat with salt and pepper. Dust with flour.
Heat oil in a skillet. Brown meat well on both sides.

3 large onions
40 g (1.5 oz) butter

Peel onions. Chop coarsely. Heat butter in a small saucepan. Sauté onions until transparent.

1 dl (½ cup) dry
white wine
1 dl (½ cup) veal stock
(s. p. 207)

Place meat and onions in layers into a fireproof casserole. Moisten with wine and veal stock. Cover casserole. Set in oven. Braise for 1½ hours. Remove meat and onions from casserole with a slotted spoon. Keep warm. Save juice for sauce.

Potato patties:
5 large potatoes
2 eggs
3 Tbs sifted flour
Salt, nutmeg
1 Tb clarified butter

Peel potatoes and quarter. Cook in lightly salted water until tender. Drain. Pass through a food mill. Beat eggs. Combine with potatoes. Blend in flour. Season with salt and nutmeg. Heat butter in a skillet. Divide potatoes into 4 portions. Place one portion into skillet. Flatten with a spatula. Sauté until a golden brown. Turn and brown second side. Remove from pan. Keep warm. Repeat process three times.

Sauce:
30 g (1 oz) butter
2 Tbs sifted flour
1 dl (½ cup) dry
white wine
2 dl (⅞ cup) beef bouillon
Meat juice
1 Tb chervil, finely chopped
Salt, freshly ground pepper

Heat butter in a saucepan. Stir in flour and brown. Moisten with wine. Cover with bouillon and meat juice. Boil down until sauce starts to thicken. Add chervil. Whisk in butter. Correct seasoning.

2 Tbs parsley,
finely chopped

Set meat and onions on lower part of plate. Place patties above. Surround meat with sauce. Garnish with parsley.

Preparation:
20 minutes
Cooking time:
2 hours
Yields 4 servings

SCHAFFHAUSER BÖLLEDÜNNE
Onion Quiche with Cold Lettuce-Vinaigrette (Schaffhausen)

200 g (7 oz) sifted flour
80 g (2.75 oz) butter
1 Tsp salt
1 Tb water
A dash of wine vinegar

Place flour in a mixing bowl. Cut butter into small pieces. Add to flour. Rub the flour and the butter rapidly between the tips of your fingers. Add salt, water and vinegar. Knead into a smooth dough. Chill for 30 minutes. Preheat oven to 200°C (390°F).

4 large onions
40 g (1.5 oz) butter
80 g (2.75 oz) diced bacon
4 dl (1¾ cups) whippping cream
1 Tb corn starch
2 Tbs whipping cream
Salt, freshly ground pepper
2 eggs

Slice the onions finely. Heat butter and sauté onions until transparent. Remove from pan and set aside. In the same pan sauté bacon and return onions to pan. Moisten with cream. Simmer for 10 minutes. Blend corn starch with 2 Tbs cream and stir into onion mixture. Bring to a boil. Season with salt and pepper. Let cool. Beat the eggs and stir into cold mixture.

Butter for the baking sheet
Flour for dusting

Butter a baking sheet (26 cm [10¼ inches] in diameter) and dust with flour. Roll out the dough and line the baking sheet. Spread with onion mixture. Bake for 40 minutes.

Salad dressing:
1 small head green lettuce
1 dl (½ cup) whipping cream
1 bunch fresh sweet basil
Salt
1 Tb mayonnaise

Clean, trim and wash lettuce. Purée in a blender with cream and basil. Rub through a fine sieve. Correct seasoning. Stir in the mayonnaise. Serve in a sauce boat accompanying the onion quiche.

Preparation:
1 hour
Cooking time:
45 minutes
Yields 4 servings

TESSINER KALBFLEISCHVÖGEL
Stuffed Escalopes of Veal with Merlot-Risotto (Ticino)

Preparation:
1 hour
Cooking time:
50 minutes
Yields 4 servings

Escalopes:
300 g (10.5 oz) caul of pork
1 Tb dried ceps for the
sauce

Soak the caul in cold water. Soak the ceps in cold water.

250 g (8.75 oz) lean veal
2 egg whites
1 dl (½ cup) whipping
cream

Cut the veal into cubes. Divide into small portions and purée in a blender by adding some egg white and cream.

60 g (2 oz) fresh ceps
1 small onion
1 Tsp parsley
15 g (0.5 oz) butter

Clean, trim and chop the ceps. Chop onion and parsley finely. Heat butter. Sauté ceps and onions. Add parsley and sauté briefly. Let cool. Combine with meat mixture and blend well. Season with salt and pepper. Chill.

8 thin escalopes of veal
about 50 g (1.75 oz) each
Salt, freshly ground pepper
1 Tb cooking-oil

Pound the escalopes until very thin. Season with salt and pepper. Spread with stuffing to a thickness of 4–5 mm (³⁄₁₆ inch). Roll up tightly. Drain the caul thoroughly. Spread out on the table and cut 8 squares 10x15 cm (4x6 inches). Wrap the stuffed escalopes. Preheat oven to 120°C (250°F).

Sauce:
Dried ceps (see above)
1 small onion
1 clove garlic
10 g (0.5 oz) butter
1 Tsp tomato paste
1 dl (½ cup) Merlot
2 dl (⅞ cup) veal stock
(s. p. 207)
30 g (1 oz) butter
Salt, freshly ground pepper
1 Tb cooking-oil

Drain ceps well. Chop onion. Mash garlic. Heat butter and sauté onions and garlic. Stir in tomato paste and ceps. Mix well. Moisten with Merlot and bring to a boil. Cover with veal stock. Bring to a simmer and boil sauce down to half its volume. Strain through fine sieve and return to saucepan. Bring back to a boil and whisk in the butter. Season with salt and pepper. Keep warm.
Heat oil in a heavy pan. Sear stuffed escalopes well on all sides. Set pan in the oven for 25 minutes.

Merlot-Risotto:
1 small onion
10 g (0.5 oz) butter
80 g (2.75 oz) risotto rice,
unpolished
2 dl (⅞ cup) Merlot
3 dl (1¼ cups) meat
bouillon
30 g (1 oz) butter
2 Tbs Parmesan, grated
Salt, freshly ground pepper
1 Tsp thyme leaves

Chop onion finely. Heat butter and sauté onions. Add the rice and stir well. Moisten with Merlot and cover with bouillon. Bring to a simmer and cook until tender. Stir continuously. Stir in the butter and cheese. Season with salt, pepper and thyme.

4 twigs thyme

Place the risotto on the upper-part of the plate. Dry the stuffed escalopes with a paper towel. Slice diagonally and arrange below the risotto. Surround with sauce and decorate with a twig of thyme.

BERNER HEITISTURM

Blueberries with Cinnamon Croûtons and Sour Cream Ice-Cream (Berne)

Ice-Cream:
1 dl (½ cup) water
250 g (8.75 oz) granulated sugar
5 dl (2⅛ cup) sour cream

In a saucepan bring water and sugar to a boil. Let cool. Stir in sour cream. Freeze.

Preparation:
10 minutes
Cooking time:
20 minutes
Yields 4 servings

Blueberries:
80 g (2.75 oz) white bread
100 g (3.5 oz) butter
50 g (1.75 oz) sifted flour

Remove rind from bread. Cut slices into small cubes. Heat 50 g (1.75 oz) butter. Fry bread cubes until crisp. Set aside. In the same pan heat remaining butter until a light brown. Stir in the flour and brown. Let cool.

800 g (1¾ lbs) blueberries
150 g (5.5 oz) granulated sugar
1 Tsp ground cinnamon
2 dl (⅞ cup) heavy cream
1 dl (½ cup) whipping cream

Wash blueberries. Combine croûtons, sugar, cinnamon and heavy cream with browned flour. Whip cream until stiff. Carefully fold into mixture.

100 g (3.5 oz) blueberries
1 bunch fresh mint leaves
Confectioner's sugar

Place blueberry mixture in soup plates. Scoop ice-cream with two hot tablespoons and place in center of blueberries. Sprinkle with fresh blueberries, garnish with mint leaves and dust with confectioner's sugar.

BROMBEERGRATIN
Blackberries au Gratin with Curd Cheese and Red Currant Sherbert

Sherbert:
500 g (1 lb) red currants
100 g (3.5 oz) granulated sugar
2 dl (⅞ cup) fruity white wine
0.5 dl (¼ cup) water
1 egg white

Wash the red currants and remove stems. Place in a saucepan. Add sugar, water and wine. Bring to a boil. Purée in a blender and strain through a fine sieve. Let cool. Beat the egg white lightly and stir into purée. Freeze.
Preheat oven to 200°C (390°F).

Preparation:
15 minutes
Cooking time:
8–10 minutes
Yields 4 servings

Blackberry gratin:
600 g (1¼ lbs) black-berries
1 egg yolk
2 Tbs vanilla sugar
10 g (0.25 oz) butter
200 g (7 oz) curd cheese or ricotta
45 g (1.5 oz) granulated sugar
Grated rind of ½ orange
Grated rind of ½ lemon
4 Tbs kirsch
2 egg whites
45 g (1.5 oz) granulated sugar

Sprinkle the blackberries with vanilla sugar. Butter 4 small gratin dishes. Spread with blackberries. Beat the curd or ricotta. Add the sugar, orange- and lemon rinds and the kirsch. Mix well. Beat the egg whites with the sugar. Fold into curd mixture. Spread over blackberries. Broil (gratinate) for 8–10 minutes.

20 pistachio nuts, shelled

Chop the pistachio nuts coarsely.

1 bunch lemon balm
Confectioner's sugar

To serve top the gratin with red currant sherbert or serve separately. Dust with confectioner's sugar, sprinkle with pistachio nuts and garnish with lemon balm.

CLAFOUTIS
Cherry Flan with Cherry Ice-Cream and Pralin (Jura)

Cherry ice-cream:
300 g (9.5 oz) cherries
3 dl (1¼ cups) milk
2 Tbs kirsch
4 egg yolks
80 g (2.75 oz) granulated sugar
2 dl (⅞ cup) whipping cream

Wash and pit the cherries. Purée in a blender with 1.5 dl (⅔ cup) milk. Rub through a sieve. Bring remaining milk and cream to a boil. In a bowl combine eggs and sugar. Beat until light and lemon-colored. Gradually stir in the hot liquid. Return to saucepan. Beat over low heat until it thickens. Do not boil! Let cool. Blend with puréed cherries. Freeze.

Pralin:
4 Tbs granulated sugar
4 Tbs ground almonds

Caramelize sugar in a small saucepan. Add the almonds and stir well. Rinse a stainless steel or marble surface with cold water. Turn the pralin onto this surface and let cool. Chop finely with a knife.
Preheat oven to 180°C (356°F).

Flan:
700 g (1½ lbs) cherries
50 g (1.75 oz) granulated sugar
2 dl (⅞ cup) milk
2 Tbs sifted flour
100 g (3.5 oz) curd cheese
1½ vanilla beans, seeds scraped
2 eggs
3 Tbs kirsch
10 g (0.25 oz) butter

Wash and pit the cherries. Transfer to a mixing bowl. Stir in sugar, milk, flour, cream, curd and vanilla seeds. Beat the eggs and add to mixture. Stir in the kirsch. Butter 4 small gratin dishes. Fill with the mixture. Bake for 25 minutes or until golden brown.

Confectioner's sugar

Scoop the ice-cream with two hot tablespoons and place in center of flan. Dust with confectioner's sugar and sprinkle with pralin.

Preparation:
20 minutes
Cooking time:
30 minutes
Yields 4 servings

GEDÜNSTETE PFLAUMEN
Stewed Plums in Honey with Cinnamon Ice-Cream

Ice-cream:
1 dl (½ cup) milk
3 dl (1¼ cups) whipping cream
½ stick cinnamon
2 Tsp ground cinnamon
1 vanilla bean, slit open

In a small saucepan combine milk, cream, cinnamon and vanilla bean. Bring to a boil.

Preparation:
25 minutes
Cooking time:
25 minutes
Yields 4 servings

80 g (2.75 oz) granulated sugar
3 egg yolks

In a bowl beat egg yolks and sugar until light and lemon-colored. Gradually stir in the hot liquid. Return to pan. Over low heat beat until cream thickens. Do not boil! Remove spices. Let cool. Freeze.

Plums:
600 g (1½ lbs) fresh plums
150 g (5.25 oz) granulated sugar
7 dl (3 cups) red wine (Dôle)
0.5 dl (¼ cup) kirsch
1 Tb pine kernels
1 Tb pistachio nuts, peeled
2 Tbs dark honey
1 dl (½ cup) black currant liqueur (Cassis)
½ lemon, juice

Wash, halve and pit the plums. In a saucepan caramelize sugar. Add plums and stir well. Moisten with wine and kirsch. Add pine kernels, pistachio nuts, honey and liqueur. Simmer for 10 minutes. Strain plums. Collect juice. Transfer to a small saucepan. Add lemon juice and boil sauce down to half its volume. Return plums to sauce. Simmer gently for 15 minutes.

1 bunch fresh mint leaves

Arrange plums and sauce in a soup plate. Top with cinnamon ice-cream. Garnish with fresh mint. The plums can be served warm as well as cold.

LUZERNER CHRIESISUPPE
Cherry Soup with Cinnamon Croûtons (Lucerne)

1 kg (2 lbs) cherries
40 g (1.5 oz) granulated sugar
0.5 dl (¼ cup) dry white wine
1 dl (½ cup) water
2 dl (⅞ cup) whipping cream
2 sheets gelatin
1 vanilla bean, slit open
40 g (1.5 oz) granulated sugar
2 Tbs kirsch

Wash and pit cherries. Caramelize sugar in a saucepan. Add cherries and turn well. Moisten with wine. Cover with water and cream. Soak the gelatin in little water. Stir sugar and vanilla bean into cherries. Simmer for 15 minutes. Remove vanilla bean. Purée cherries in a blender and rub through a fine sieve. Drain gelatin, stir into fruit mixture and let dissolve. Add the kirsch. Fill the cherry soup into cups. Chill.

2 slices white bread
20 g (0.75 oz) butter
15 g (0.5 oz) granulated sugar
1 Tsp ground cinnamon

Remove the rind from the bread. Cut slices into small cubes. Heat the butter. Sauté bread until crisp. Sprinkle with sugar and cinnamon. Remove from pan.

1 bunch fresh mint leaves

Top the cherry soup with croûtons and mint leaves.

Preparation:
20 minutes
Cooking time:
15 minutes
Yields 4 servings

MALAKOFF VON BASLER LECKERLI

Malakoff of Basle Honey Cookies
with Cherry-Mousse, Stewed Cherries and Vanilla Ice-Cream (Basle)

**16 Basler Leckerli
(Basle honey cookies)**

Cherry-Mousse:
4 sheets gelatin
300 g (10.5 oz) ripe cherries
1 dl (½ cup) water
2 Tbs kirsch
**100 g (3.5 oz) granulated
sugar**
**2 dl (⅞ cup) whipping
cream**

Vanilla ice-cream:
3 dl (1¼ cups) milk
**2 dl (⅞ cup) whipping
cream**
3 vanilla beans, slit open
4 egg yolks
**120 g (4.25 oz) granulated
sugar**

Stewed cherries:
300 g (10.5 oz) ripe cherries
**120 g (4.25 oz) granulated
sugar**
2 dl (⅞ cup) red wine
**Coarsely ground black
pepper**

Cut the cookies crosswise. Only the frosted part will be used.

Soak gelatin in little water. Wash and pit cherries. Place in a blender. Add water and kirsch. Purée and rub through a fine sieve. Stir in sugar. Blend well. Drain gelatin well. Place in a small saucepan. Let dissolve over low heat. Stir into cherry mixture. Whip cream until stiff. Fold into purée. Transfer to a bowl. Let settle in the refrigerator for at least 2 hours.

In a saucepan bring milk, cream and vanilla beans to the boil. Beat egg yolks and sugar until light and lemon-colored. Gradually stir in hot liquid. Return to saucepan. Stir continuously until custard thickens. Let cool. Freeze.

Wash and pit cherries. In a saucepan caramelize sugar until a light brown. Add cherries. Turn well. Moisten with wine. Simmer for 5 minutes. Season with a pinch of black pepper.

Place cookies on a baking sheet. Spread 12 with a 1 cm (⅜ inch) cherry mousse. Place 3 on top of each other. Repeat procedure four times. Cover with remaining cookies. Transfer malakoffs onto plates. Arrange with stewed cherries and vanilla ice-cream.

Preparation:
25 minutes
Cooking time:
35 minutes
Yields 4 servings

SEELÄNDER MEERTRÜBELCHUECHE
Red Currant Tart with Stewed Berries

200 g (7 oz) puff pastry or sweet short paste
Butter for the cake pan
Flour

Butter a false-bottomed cake pan 26 cm (10¼ inches) in diameter. Dust with flour. Roll out dough to a thickness of 3 mm (⅛ inch). Line cake pan. Prick with a fork. Chill for 30 minutes.

Filling:
2 egg yolks
200 g (7 oz) granulated sugar
100 g (3.5 oz) cream cheese
2 dl (⅞ cup) whipping cream
250 g (8.75 oz) red currants
250 g (8.75 oz) blueberries
2 egg whites

Preheat oven to 200°C (390°F).
In a mixing bowl beat egg yolks and sugar until light and lemon-colored. Whip cream. Fold into mixture. Remove stems from red currants. Blend red currants and blueberries with mixture. Beat egg white until stiff. Fold into fruit mixture. Fill into prepared cake pan. Bake for 30–40 minutes.

Stewed berries:
100 g (3.5 oz) blueberries
200 g (7 oz) red currants
120 g (4.25 oz) hazelnuts, ground
60 g (2 oz) granulated sugar
0.5 dl (¼ cup) dry white wine

Remove stems from red currants. In a small saucepan caramelize sugar until a light brown. Stir in hazelnuts and brown. Add red currants and blueberries. Stir well. Moisten with wine. Cook for about 5 minutes.

Confectioner's sugar

Unmold tart. Let cool on a rack. Dust with confectioner's sugar. Cut into serving pieces. Arrange tart and berries on plates.

Preparation:
15 minutes
Cooking time:
1 hour
Yields 8 servings

BÜNDNER GERSTENSUPPE
Barley Soup with Lamb (Grisons)

1 small onion
50 g (1.75 oz) knob celery
1 carrot
½ leek
60 g (2 oz) air-dried beef
or smoked bacon
40 g (1.5 oz) pearl barley
30 g (1 oz) butter
1 dl (½ cup) dry
white wine
2 l (8 cups) beef bouillon

Chop onion finely. Clean, trim, wash and dice vegetables. Dice beef or bacon. Heat butter in a large saucepan. Sauté onions and vegetables. Add barley and beef. Sauté briefly. Moisten with wine. Cover with bouillon. Bring to the boil. Simmer for 1½ hours.

Preparation:
20 minutes
Cooking time:
2 hours
Yields 4 servings

2 dl (⅞ cup) whipping
cream
40 g (1.5 oz) butter
Salt, freshly ground pepper

Purée soup in a blender. Rub through a sieve. Return to saucepan. Stir in cream and butter. Season with salt and pepper. Keep warm.

1 small carrot
½ leek
40 g (1.5 oz) knob celery
30 g (1 oz) pearl barley

Clean, trim, wash and dice carrot, leek and celery. Fill a saucepan with water. Add salt. Bring to the boil. Add barley and vegetables. Cook «al dente».

160 g (5.5 oz) lamb sirloin
Salt, freshly ground pepper
1 Tb clarified butter

Season lamb. Heat clarified butter. Sear meat on both sides for 3 minutes. Do not overcook!

50 g (1.75 oz) air-dried beef
1 bunch marjoram

Dice beef. Transfer beef, barley and vegetables into soup plates. Cover with soup. Slice lamb thinly. Add to soup. Garnish with marjoram.

LINSENSÜPPCHEN
Lentil Soup with Small Liver Dumplings

1 small onion
30 g (1 oz) bacon
¼ leek
20 g (0.75 oz) butter
80 g (2.75 oz) yellow lentils
1.2 l (5 cups) chicken broth
Salt, freshly ground white pepper

Chop onion finely. Dice bacon and leek. In a saucepan heat the butter. Sauté onions and bacon well. Add leeks and lentils. Sauté for a moment. Moisten with bouillon. Bring to a boil. Simmer for 2½ hours.

Preparation:
20 minutes
Cooking time:
2 hours 30 minutes
Yields 4 servings

Liver dumplings:
100 g (3.5 oz) chicken liver
40 g (1.5 oz) butter
80 g (2.75 oz) white bred, stale, grated
2 egg yolks
1 egg white

Skin the liver. Press through a fine sieve. Beat butter until smooth. Add the liver and mix well. Stir in egg yolks and bread crumbs. Season with salt and pepper. Beat the egg white until stiff. Fold into liver mixture. In a skillet bring water to a simmer. Add salt. Form dumplings with two teaspoons and poach for 5 minutes. Remove from water and place in a kettle filled with cold water.

1 dl (½ cup) whipping cream

In a blender purée the soup. Strain through a sieve and return to saucepan. Add the cream. Bring to a boil. Correct seasoning. Add the dumplings and reheat. Serve.

MURTENER KÜRBISSCHAUMSUPPE
Pumpkin Froth Soup

1.8 kg (4 lbs) pumpkin (net weight 900 g [2 lbs])
1 onion
1 carrot
½ leek
50 g (1.75 oz) butter
50 g (1.75 oz) slivered almonds
2 dl (7/8 cup) bouillon
2 dl (7/8 cup) milk
2 dl (7/8 cup) whipping cream

Cut pumpkin, onion and vegetables into small pieces. Heat butter in a large saucepan. Sauté vegetables until slightly golden. Add almonds. Stir well. Moisten with bouillon. Stir in milk and cream. Bring to the boil. Reduce heat and simmer for 1 hour 20 minutes.

Preparation:
15 minutes
Cooking time:
1 hour 20 minutes
Yields 10 servings

Salt, freshly ground pepper
30 g (1 oz) butter
2 Tbs whipped cream

Purée soup in a blender. Rub through a fine sieve. Return to saucepan. Bring to the boil. Season with salt and pepper. Stir in butter. Fold in whipped cream.

1 Tbs slivered almonds
1 twig chervil

Roast the almonds until a light brown. Pour soup into cups. Sprinkle with almonds. Garnish with chervil.

TESSINER MINESTRONE
Minestrone (Ticino)

40 g (1.5 oz) Borlotti beans

Soak Borlotti beans overnight.
Drain the beans.

1 onion
2 carrots
1 leek
60 g (2 oz) knob celery
100 g (3.5 oz) potatoes
¼ white cabbage
2 cloves garlic
1 Tb olive oil
30 g (1 oz) bacon, diced
4–5 rosemary leaves
1 twig thyme
1 twig marjoram
1 Tb tomato paste
0.5 dl (¼ cup) red wine
1.6 l (6¾ cups) bouillon

Clean, trim and wash vegetables. Slice finely. Chop onion finely. Mash garlic. Heat oil in a large saucepan. Sauté bacon. Add onions, garlic, vegetables and herbs. Sauté briefly. Add tomato paste. Stir well. Add beans. Moisten with wine. Cover with bouillon. Bring to the boil. Simmer for 15 minutes. Strain soup through a fine sieve. Set beans and vegetables aside.

20 g (0.75 oz) Italian rice
15 g (0.5 oz) spaghetti

Bring bouillon back to the boil. Add rice. Cook for 8–10 minutes. Break spaghetti and add to bouillon. Cook «al dente» for 10–12 minutes.

2 tomatoes

Skin, quarter and seed tomatoes. Dice.

Salt, freshly ground pepper
30 g (1 oz) Parmesan, grated

Return beans and vegetables to bouillon. Bring to the boil. Stir in diced tomatoes. Season with salt and pepper. Serve in soup cups. Sprinkle with Parmesan.

Preparation:
20 minutes
Cooking time:
1 hour
Yields 6 servings

BASLER LAUBFRÖSCH
Stuffed Spinach on Savoy Cabbage (Basle)

Stuffing:
1 carrot
30 g (1 oz) knob celery
1 onion
1 Tb cooking-oil
300 g (10.5 oz) ground beef
200 g (7 oz) ground veal
2 Tbs tomato paste
1–2 Tbs sifted flour
1 dl (½ cup) veal stock
(s. p. 207)
1 dl (½ cup) red wine

Wash, trim and finely chop the vegetables. Chop onion finely. Heat the oil. Sauté the vegetables. Add the meat and tomato paste. Sauté for a moment. Dust with flour and moisten with red wine. Cover with veal stock and stir well. Let simmer over low heat until liquid has evaporated.

2 eggs
0.5 dl (¼ cup) all-purpose cream
Salt, freshly ground pepper

Transfer mixture to a bowl. Mix in eggs and cream. Season with salt and pepper. Let cool.
Preheat oven to 200°C (390°F).

500 g (1 lb) fresh large-leaved spinach
Butter for the bakingsheet

Remove stems and wash spinach. Fill a large kettle with water. Add salt. Bring to the boil. Blanch the spinach for 5 seconds. Drain carefully. Rind under running cold water. Spread one by one the leaves on a dish towel. Place 2 Tbs of stuffing on each leaf. Wrap into a little package.
Butter a bakingsheet. Place the stuffed leaves on the bakingsheet. Bake for 15 minutes.

Cabbage:
800 g (1¾ lbs) savoy cabbage
30 g (1 oz) butter
1 onion
50 g (1¾ oz) diced bacon
2 dl (⅞ cup) vegetable bouillon (s. p. 205)

Wash and trim the cabbage. Cut into very thin strips. Chop the onion. Heat the butter. Sauté onions and bacon. Add the cabbage and stir well. Moisten with bouillon and let simmer until all liquid has evapo- rated.

Sauce:
15 g (½ oz) butter
1 twig rosemary
1 twig thyme
1.5 dl (⅔ cup) red wine
2.5 dl (1 cup) veal stock
(s. p. 207)
40 g (1.5 oz) butter

Remove the stems from the herbs. Heat the butter. Sauté until butter is of a light brown color. Moisten with wine and cover with veal stock. Boil sauce down by one third. Whisk in butter.

1 large twig parsley

Place some cabbage in the centre of each plate. Top with stuffed spinach. Surround with sauce and garnish with parsley.

BERNERZÜPFE
Bernese Plait and Plum Jam with Walnuts (Berne)

20 g (0.75 oz) pressed yeast
1 Tb granulated sugar

Blend yeast and sugar in a cup. Let stand for 5 minutes.

60 g (2 oz) butter
2 dl (⅞ cup) milk

In a saucepan melt butter and add milk. Heat to lukewarm.

500 g (17 oz) sifted flour
½ Tsp salt
3 egg yolks

Place flour in a mixing bowl. Mix in salt. Make a well in the center. Add yeast, milk and eggs. Mix well. Knead into a smooth dough. Cover bowl with a damp cloth. Let dough rise to twice its volume.
Heat oven to 180°C (356°F).

1 egg yolk

Divide dough into two equal portions. Roll into two long strings and plait. Let rise for 10 minutes more. Brush with egg yolk. Chill for 10 minutes. Bake for 30–40 minutes.

Plum jam with walnuts:
2 kg (2 lbs) ripe plums
1 dl (½ cup) water
0.5 dl (¼ cup) lemon juice
2 tsp grated lemon rind
80 g (2.75 oz) raisins

Wash, pit and quarter plums. Place plums in a saucepan. Cover with water. Add lemon juice, lemon rind and raisins. Stir well. Bring to the boil. Remove from heat source. Let stand.

120 g (4.25 oz) walnuts, shelled
1 kg (2 lbs) preserving sugar
2 dl (⅞ cup) water

Quarter walnuts. In a saucepan bring water to the boil. Add walnuts. Simmer for 1 minute. Drain well. Combine plums with walnuts and preserving sugar. Cook over high heat for 3 minutes. Fill into hot, sterile jars and screw lid on immediately.

Preparation:
1 hour 30 minutes
Cooking time:
30–40 minutes
Yields 4 servings

BLUTWÜRSTLI
Blood Sausages (Black Pudding) on Sauerkraut with Pears

Sausage filling:
100 g (3.5 oz) leek
1 small onion
30 g (1 oz) butter
4 dl (1¾ cups) milk
1.6 dl (⅔ cup) heavy cream
8 g (0.25 oz) salt
Freshly ground pepper
1 Tsp sweet paprika
1 Tsp marjoram, finely
chopped
1 pinch nutmeg
6 dl (2½ cups) fresh pork
blood (order from the
butcher)
100 g (3.5 oz) beef tongue
50 g (1.75 oz) fresh pork fat
or fat salt pork,
simmered for 10 minutes
100 g (3.5 oz) pig's knuck-
les, cooked
80 g (2.75 oz) pearl barley,
cooked
4 m (4.5 yards) sausage
casing, soaked and drained

Chop onion and leek finely. In a large skillet heat the butter. Sauté onions and leeks. Moisten with milk. Bring to a boil. Remove pan from heat source and stir in the cream. Season with salt, pepper, paprika, nutmeg and marjoram. Mix well. Add the blood, stirring vigorously. Dice tongue, pork fat, knuckle and add to mixture. Stir in barley. Blend well. With a funnel fill the sausage casing. Tie 2 knots every 7–8 cm (2¾ inches), so sausages can be separated. Fill a large kettle with water. Heat to 80°C (176°F). Add salt. Poach the sausages for 40 minutes.

Sauerkraut:
2 onions
80 g (2.75 oz) slab bacon
20 g (0.75 oz) butter
400 g (1 lb) sauerkraut
1 dl (½ cup) dry
white wine
Salt, freshly ground pepper

Chop onions finely. Dice bacon. Heat the butter in a saucepan. Sauté onions and bacon. Stir in sauerkraut and sauté briefly. Moisten with wine. Cook for 12 minutes. Season with salt and little pepper.

Pears:
3 unblemished pears
50 g (1.75 oz) granulated
sugar
1 dl (½ cup) water

Peel and core the pears. Slice into wedges. In a small saucepan caramelize sugar. Moisten with water. Add the pears. Cook over low heat for about 8 minutes. Set aside.

Sauce:
2 dl (⅞ cup) veal stock
(s. p. 207)
2 dl (⅞ cup) red wine
30 g (1 oz) butter
Salt

In a small saucepan combine veal stock and wine. Boil down to half its volume. Whisk in the butter. Season with salt.

1 twig parsley

In the center of the serving plates form small sauerkrautpedestals. Set the sausages on top and the pears on both sides. Spoon sauce around sauerkraut. Garnish with parsley.

Preparation:
1 hour
Cooking time:
1 hour
Yields 4 servings

116

BRASATO AL MERLOT
Beef Braised in Merlot with Herb-Risotto

1 kg (2 lbs) beef
(London broil, shank)
Salt, freshly ground pepper

½ leek
2 carrots
4 Tbs olive oil
1 Tb tomato paste
30 g (1 oz) dried ceps
2 Tbs sifted flour
5 dl (2⅛ cups) Merlot
50 g (1.75 oz) raisins
1 bay leaf
1 twig rosemary
1.5 dl (⅔ cup) veal stock
(s. p. 207)
1 l (4¼ cups) beef bouillon
40 g (1.5 oz) butter

Risotto:
20 g (0.75 oz) butter
1 onion, finely chopped
140 g (5 oz) Italian rice
1 dl (½ cup) dry
white wine
3 dl (1¼ cups) bouillon
0.5 dl (¼ cup) whipping
cream
30 g (1 oz) butter
2 Tbs whipped cream
Salt
1 Tsp chervil, finely
chopped
1 Tsp sweet basil, finely
chopped
½ Tsp thyme leaves
1 Tsp parsley, finely
chopped

200 g (7 oz) chanterelles,
cleaned, trimmed
10 g (0.25 oz) butter
Salt, freshly ground pepper

Season meat with salt and pepper.
Soak ceps in little water.
Preheat oven to 180°C (356°F).

Clean, trim and dice vegetables. In a fireproof casserole heat oil and brown meat well on all sides. Add vegetables and sauté briefly. Stir in tomato paste. Drain ceps well. Add to casserole. Dust with flour. Moisten with wine. Stir in raisins and spices. Moisten with veal stock. Cover with bouillon. Place lid on casserole. Set in oven. Braise meat for 2 hours. Remove meat from pan. Keep warm. Strain sauce through a fine sieve into a small saucepan. Bring to the boil. Whisk in butter. Correct seasoning. Keep warm.

Heat butter in a saucepan. Sauté onions. Stir in rice. Sauté until transparent. Moisten with wine. Cover with bouillon. Cook over low heat for about 20 minutes stirring continuously. Add bouillon if necessary. Stir in cream and herbs. Fold in whipped cream. Correct seasoning.

Heat butter in a skillet. Sauté chanterelles. Season with salt and pepper.

Slice meat into serving portions. Arrange meat and risotto on plates. Sprinkle with chanterelles.

Preparation:
30 minutes
Cooking time:
2 hours
Yields 4 servings

BÜNDNER BECKIBRATEN
Braised Leg of Lamb with Maluns (Grisons)

1.4 kg (3 lbs) leg of lamb, boned
Salt, freshly ground pepper
4 cloves garlic, mashed

Preheat oven to 220°C (428°F).
Season meat with salt and pepper. Rub with garlic.

2 Tbs cooking-oil
2 shallots
1 knob celery
8 carrots
4 dl (1¾ cups) red wine
5 dl (2⅛ cups) beef bouillon
1 clove
1 large twig rosemary
1 large twig thyme

Clean, trim and dice vegetables. Heat oil in a fire-proof casserole. Brown meat well on all sides for 40 minutes. Add vegetables. Sauté for 15 minutes. Moisten with wine. Cover with bouillon. Add spices and herbs. Cover casserole. Set in oven. Braise meat for 1 hour. Remove meat from pan. Keep warm. Strain juice through a fine sieve. Set aside and save for sauce.

Maluns:
1 kg (2 lbs) potatoes
400 g (14 oz) sifted flour
Salt
50 g (1.75 oz) melted butter
30 g (1 oz) butter

Peel potatoes and grate (using a grater with fairly large wholes). In a mixing bowl combine potatoes and flour. Rub the potatoes and flour together between the tips of your fingers. Blend with melted butter. Season with salt and pepper.
In a skillet heat butter. Place the potato mixture into pan and brown. The mixture will break into small pieces.

Sauce:
20 g (0.75 oz) butter
10 g (0.25 oz) sifted flour
5 dl meat juice
30 g (1 oz) butter
Salt, freshly ground pepper

Heat butter in a small saucepan. Stir in flour and brown slightly. Gradually stir in meat juice. Stir until smooth and boil down to half its volume. Whisk in butter. Correct seasoning.

Cut meat into slices 5 mm (³⁄₁₆ inch) thick. Set on lower part of plates. Spread Maluns over meat. Surround with sauce.
As a side dish serve glazed carrots, zucchini and knob celery.

Preparation:
25 minutes
Cooking time:
2 hours 30 minutes
Yields 4 servings

BÜNDNER CAPUNS
Stuffed Swiss Chard

250 g (8.75 oz) sifted flour
3 eggs
1 dl (½ cup) milk
1 Tb salt

Place flour in a bowl. Beat eggs and blend with milk. Add salt. Stir into flour and mix well.

1 smoked pork sausage
60 g (2 oz) air-dried beef
60 g (2 oz) salted and smoked ham
1 Tb parsley, finely chopped
Salt, freshly ground pepper

Dice the meat. Add to flour mixture. Stir in parsley. Season with salt and pepper. Work into a smooth batter.

20 g (0.75 oz) butter
1 onion

Chop onion finely. In a small pan heat the butter. Sauté onion. Mix into batter.

16 large leaves of Swiss chard
30 g (1 oz) butter
1 dl (½ cup) milk
0.5 dl (¼ cup) beef bouillon

Fill a large kettle with water. Add salt. Bring to the boil. Wash the chard leaves and blanch until wilted. Drain. Spread one by one on a clean towel. Remove the stalks with a knife. Place some batter on each leaf and roll up lengthwise. In a frying pan heat the butter. Braise the Capuns. Moisten with milk and bouillon. Cover and let simmer for 15 minutes.

30 g (1 oz) Raclette cheese, grated
50 g (1.75 oz) diced bacon

Remove the Capuns from the pan. Drain well. Transfer to a warm platter. Spinkle with cheese. Heat the butter until a light-brown. Add the bacon and sauté. Pour over the Capuns.

Preparation:
20 minutes
Cooking time:
30 minutes
Yields 4 servings

FALSCHE FROSCHSCHENKELI
False «Frog Legs» on Tomato Sauce

1 large onion
20 g (0.75 oz) butter
2 Tbs tomato paste

Chop onion finely. In a large saucepan heat butter. Sauté onions. Stir in tomato paste. Mix well. Let cool.

1 Tb parsley
2 eggs
400 g (1 lb) cold meat (leftovers), ground
100 g (3.5 oz) bread crumbs
Salt, freshly ground black pepper
2 big pinches nutmeg
Butter for the baking sheet

Chop parsley finely. Beat eggs. In a bowl mix meat, eggs and parsley. Add bread crumbs. Stir in onion mixture. Season with salt, pepper and nutmeg. Blend well. Butter a baking sheet. Spread the mixture on baking sheet to a thickness of 1 cm (⅜ inch). Chill.

Tomato sauce:
1 kg (2¼ lbs) tomatoes
2 onions
1 clove garlic
0.4 dl (¼ cup) olive oil
100 g (3.5 oz) bacon, sliced
1 twig rosemary
1 dl (½ cup) red wine
Salt, freshly ground pepper
1 clove garlic

Remove stems from tomatoes. Cut into small pieces. Chop onions and garlic coarsley. In a saucepan heat oil. Sauté onions, garlic and bacon well. Add rosemary. Stir in tomato paste. Mix well. Moisten with wine. Cover pan and simmer for 2 hours. Remove rosemary and purée tomatoes in a blender. Season with salt and pepper. Mash garlic and add to sauce. Keep warm.

Batter:
2 eggs
1 dl (½ cup) beer
30 g (1 oz) melted butter
100 g (3.5 oz) sifted flour

In a mixing bowl beat eggs. Stir in butter and beer. Gradually stir in flour. Work into a smooth and creamy batter. Season with salt.

Oil for deep-frying

Heat oil for frying.
Cut the meat mixture into sticks the size of a middle finger. Turn in flour and dip in batter. Deep-fry until crisp. Drain on paper towel. Reheat tomato sauce.

1 bunch chervil

Pour some sauce on each plate. Set the «false frogs» in center. Garnish with chervil.

Preparation:
1 hour
Cooking time:
2 hours 10 minutes
Yields 4 servings

GEFÜLLTE ZWIEBELN
Stuffed Onions on Leeks

4 large yellow (Spanish) onions
15 g (½ oz) butter
1 dl (½ cup) chicken broth
Butter for the gratin dish

Preheat oven to 180°C (356°F).
Peel onions. Set in buttered gratin dish. Moisten with broth. Bake for 45 minutes. Remove onions from the dish. Cut off a thick slice from the top of each onion. Scoop out the center to form cups. Chop the top slices and onion centers. Set aside.

Stuffing:
1 onion
¼ leek
20 g (¾ oz) butter
500 g (1 lb) ground chicken meat
1 Tb sifted flour
1 dl (½ cup) heavy cream
Salt, freshly ground pepper
1 Tsp sweet paprika
1 Tb chervil, finely chopped
30 g (1 oz) Gruyère, grated

Chop onion finely. Dice leeks. Heat the butter and sauté the onions until golden brown. Stir in the leeks and the ground chicken. Mix well and sauté briefly. Dust with flour. Moisten with chicken stock and cover with cream. Bring to the simmer. Season with salt, pepper, paprika and chervil. Boil over low heat for about 10 minutes, or, until sauce reaches a creamy consistency. Add chopped onions. Stuff the onion cups with the mixture. Place in gratin dish. Sprinkle with cheese. Bake until golden brown.

Leeks:
3 medium size leeks
20 g (¾ oz) butter
2 dl (⅞ cup) all whipping cream
Salt, freshly ground pepper

Halve the leeks lengthwise. Wash and cut into long strips. Heat the butter and sauté the leeks. Moisten with cream and bring to a boil. Reduce temperature and cook leeks for 30 minutes. Stir continuously to prevent sticking. Season with salt and pepper. Set aside and keep warm.

Sauce:
4 dl (1¾ cups) chicken stock
2 Tbs honey
2 Tbs wine vinegar
30 g (1 oz) butter

Bring the chicken stock to a boil and reduce over high heat to 1.5 dl (⅔ cup). Stir in the honey and the wine. Whisk in the butter. Correct seasoning. Keep warm.

2 large twigs fresh chervil

Place the leeks in centre of plate and top with a stuffed onion. Surround with sauce. Garnish with chervil.

Preparation:
15 minutes
Cooking time:
40 minutes
Yields 4 servings

GEMSPFEFFER MIT APFELSTÜCKLI
Chamois Goulash with Cooked Apples

1 kg chamois, shoulder

Cut meat into cubes of about 40 g (1.5 oz).

Marinade:
2 cloves
2 bay leaves
1 twig rosemary
2 cloves garlic, peeled, quartered
1 large onion, peeled, quartered
1 bottle red wine
1 dl (½ cup) vinegar

Place meat in an earthenware bowl. Add all the ingredients for the marinade. Mix well. Meat should always be covered with marinade. If necessary place a heavy plate on top. Marinate for 8 days.

Salt, freshly ground pepper
2 Tbs cooking oil
2 Tbs sifted flour
2 dl (⅞ cup) red wine
2 dl (⅞ cup) beef bouillon
3 dl (1¼ cups) marinade

Remove meat from marinade. Dry with a clean cloth. Strain the marinade and set aside. Season meat with salt and pepper. Heat the oil in a roasting pan. Sear the meat well on all sides. Dust with flour and brown well. Moisten with wine. Cover with bouillon and marinade. Bring to the boil. Cover and simmer for 2 hours.

½ clove garlic, mashed
2 Tbs elderberry preserve
25 g (⅞ oz) butter
Salt, freshly ground pepper

Remove meat from sauce and keep warm. Strain the sauce through a fine sieve. Add the garlic and elderberry preserve. Bring to a boil and whisk in the butter. Season with salt and pepper. Return meat to sauce. Keep warm.

Apples:
4 apples
30 g (1 oz) granulated sugar
1 dl (½ cup) dry white wine
1 stick cinnamon
1 clove

Peel and core the apples. Cut into eight wedges. In a small saucepan caramelize the sugar until a light brown. Add apples and turn well. Moisten with white wine. Add the spices. Cook over low heat until tender. Remove the spices.

1 twig fresh thyme

Place the meat in the lower half of the plates. Arrange the apples on both sides in a fan-like design. Place the side-dish above the meat. Decorate with thyme leaves.

Side dish: mashed potatoes or spaezle (german flour dumplings).

Marinating:
8 days
Preparation:
20 minutes
Cooking time:
2 hours 10 minutes
Yields 4 servings

HEIDELBEER-RISOTTO
Blueberry-Risotto with Boletus (Cèpe)

250 g (8.75 oz) fresh Boletus (Cèpe)
1 small onion
20 g (0.75 oz) butter
140 g (5 oz) risotto rice, unpolished
150 g (5.5 oz) blueberries
0.5 dl (¼ cup) dry white wine
4 dl (1¾ cups) bouillon
Salt, freshly ground pepper

Clean, trim and slice mushrooms. Set aside. Chop onion finely. In a saucepan heat the butter and sauté onions. Stir in the rice and blueberries. Sauté briefly. Moisten with wine and cover with bouillon. Cook until tender. Stir continuously. If necessary add some bouillon. Season with salt and pepper.

0.4 dl (¼ cup) olive oil
Boletus, see above
1 twig thyme
1 pinch garlic, mashed
60 g (2 oz) butter

In a skillet heat the oil. Sauté mushrooms, garlic and thyme. Stir the butter into risotto. Transfer to warm plates. Decorate with mushrooms.

Preparation:
15 minutes
Cooking time:
40 minutes
Yields 4 servings

LUZERNER CHÜGELIPASTETE
Puff Pastry with Meat Filling (Lucerne)

Filling:
1 onion
1 clove garlic
40 g (1.5 oz) butter
180 g (6.25 oz) veal (loin)
180 g (6.25 oz) pork (loin)
2 dl (⅞ cup) dry
white wine
80 g (2.75 oz) raisins

Chop onion and garlic finely. Cut meat into small cubes. Heat butter in a skillet. Sauté onions and garlic. Add meat and brown well. Moisten with wine. Add raisins. Cook over low heat for 10 minutes. Set aside.

Preparation:
30 minutes
Cooking time:
40 minutes
Yields 4 servings

200 g (7 oz) uncooked veal
sausage meat
1 l (4¼ cups) bouillon
200 g (7 oz) sweet breads

In a saucepan bring bouillon to the boil. Fill sausage meat into a pastry bag. Press small balls into simmering bouillon. Remove saucepan from heat source. Let balls cool in the broth. Remove from pan. Set aside. Reheat bouillon. Place sweet breads into liquid and poach for 20 minutes. Let cool in the broth. Trim the sweet breads and remove any filaments of fat, gristle or tubes.

100 g (3.5 oz) mushrooms
20 g (0.75 oz) butter
1 Tb sifted flour
2.5 dl (1 cup) whipping
cream
Salt, freshly ground pepper
Nutmeg

Trim, clean and slice mushrooms. In a skillet heat butter and sauté mushrooms. Dust with flour and stir well. Moisten with bouillon and bring to the boil. Remove mushrooms from liquid with a slotted spoon and set aside. Stir cream into bouillon and boil until sauce thickens to a creamy consistency. Return meat, sausage balls, sweet breads and mushrooms to sauce and stir well. Season to taste with salt, pepper and nutmeg. Let stand.

200 g puff pastry
1 egg yolk
Butter for the baking sheet

Preheat oven to 180°C (356°F).
Roll out pastry to a thickness of 3 mm (⅛ inch) and cut into a large heart. Brush with egg yolk. Place puff pastry heart on a buttered baking sheet and bake for 10–15 minutes. Let cool on a rack.

1 twig parsley

Carefully reheat filling. With a large knife halve pastry heart crosswise. Spread bottom-half with filling and cover with top. Garnish with parsley. Serve remaining filling separately.

OCHSENSCHWANZRAGOUT
Oxtail Stew with Fried Leek

1.6 kg (3½ lbs) oxtail, cut into 3 cm (1³⁄₁₆ inches) pieces
Salt, freshly ground pepper
3 Tbs sifted flour
2 Tbs cooking-oil

Season oxtail with salt and pepper. Dust with flour. Heat oil in a heavy saucepan. Brown oxtail well on all sides. Remove from pan. Set aside.

Preparation: 30 minutes
Cooking time: 3 hours
Yields 4 servings

2 carrots
½ leek
100 g (3.5 oz) knob celery
2 onions
2 cloves garlic
5 dl (2⅛ cups) red wine
5 dl (2⅛ cups) beef bouillon
2 bay leaves
1 twig thyme

Dice vegetables. Chop onions. Mash garlic. Sauté in the previously used pan. Return meat to pan. Turn well. Moisten with wine and cover with bouillon. Add the spices. Set lid on casserole and simmer for 2½–3 hours.
Prepare spaetzle.

1.5 dl (²⁄₃ cup) heavy cream
Salt, freshly ground pepper
20 g (0.75 oz) butter, chilled

Remove oxtail from pan. Let cool. Bone. Strain the sauce through a fine sieve into a small saucepan. Add cream and boil until it reaches a creamy consistency. Correct seasoning. Whisk in the butter. Keep warm.

3 leeks
100 g (3.5 oz) sifted flour
1 l (8 cups) oil for deep-frying
Salt

Heat the oil to 180°C (356°F). Slice the leeks into 2 mm (¹⁄₁₆ inch) rings. Wash and dry well. Dust generously with flour. Place in a sieve and shake. Deep-fry until golden brown. Drain on paper towel. Salt before serving.

1 bunch chives

Return oxtail to sauce. Reheat carefully. Chop the chives finely. Stir into sauce.

2 large twigs parsley

Arrange meat in center of plates. Sprinkle with fried leeks. Set the spaetzle on the side. Garnish with parsley.

Spaetzle (german dumplings) as a side dish.

SCHAFSVERDÄMPF
Lamb and Potato Stew

20 cloves garlic
2 dl (⁷⁄₈ cup) milk
Salt

Peel garlic. Heat milk. Salt lightly. Add garlic and cook «al dente». Drain.

800 g (1¾ lbs) lamb shoulder
250 g (8.75 oz) onions, coarsely chopped
2 Tbs cooking-oil
½ Tsp ground cinnamon
1 dl (½ cup) red wine
1 l (4¼ cups) bouillon
1½ stick cinnamon
Salt, freshly ground pepper

Peel onions. Slice finely. Cut the meat into 40 g (1.5 oz) cubes. Heat oil in a large saucepan. Brown meat well on all sides. Add garlic and onions and brown. Stir in ground cinnamon. Moisten with wine. Cover with bouillon. Add stick cinnamon. Season with salt and pepper.

800 g (1¾ lbs) potatoes

Peel potatoes. Cut into 1½ cm (⁹⁄₁₆ inch) cubes. Add to meat and stir well. Cover saucepan and braise for 1 hour 10 minutes. Add bouillon if necessary. Remove meat and potatoes from saucepan. Keep warm.

40 g (1.5 oz) butter
Salt, freshly ground pepper

Bring the sauce back to a boil. Stir in the butter. Correct seasoning. Keep warm.

2 leeks
1 Tbs sifted flour
Oil for deep-frying

Clean, trim and wash leeks. Slice finely. Heat the oil. Dust leeks with flour. Deep-fry until crisp. Drain on paper towel.

1 twig parsley

Place meat and potatoes in center of plates. Coat with sauce. Sprinkle with leeks. Garnish with parsley.

Preparation:
30 minutes
Cooking time:
1 hour 40 minutes
Yields 4 servings

ZUOZER REHPFEFFER
Goulash of Venison with Buckwheat Dumplings

1 kg (2 lbs) shoulder of venison

Cut meat into cubes of 40 g (1.5 oz) each.

4 black peppercorns, crushed
2 cloves
2 bay leaves
7 dl (3 cups) red wine
1 dl (½ cup) vinegar
100 g (3.5 oz) knob celery, chopped
¼ leek, finely sliced
1 onion, chopped
2 carrots, diced
4–5 juniper berries
1 twig pine

Place meat in an earthenware bowl. Add all the ingredients for the marinade. Mix well. Cover and marinate in the refrigerator for 7 days.

3 Tbs cooking-oil
Vegetables from the marinade
4 dl (1¾ cup) marinade

Preheat oven to 180°C (356°F).
Remove meat from marinade. Dry with a clean cloth. Strain the marinade and set aside. Remove spices from vegetables and set aside. Heat oil in a fireproof casserole. Divide meat into 2 portions. Sear well on all sides. Add the vegetables from the marinade and sauté briefly. Moisten with marinade. Cover casserole. Set in oven and braise meat for 1 hour 10 minutes. Remove meat from pan. Keep warm. Strain juice through a sieve. Set aside. Prepare the dumplings. See recipe on page 66.

Sauce:
10 g (0.25 oz) butter
10 g (0.25 oz) sifted flour
1 dl (½ cup) red wine
3 dl (1¼ cups) game stock (s. p. 208)
Juice from the pan
1 dl (½ cup) pork blood (order from butcher)
20 g (0.75 oz) butter
1 pinch sugar
Salt, freshly ground pepper

Heat butter in small saucepan. Stir in flour and brown. Moisten with wine. Cover with game stock and meat juice. Over high heat boil sauce down by ⅓. Stir in the blood (do not boil!). Whisk in the butter. Season with sugar, salt and pepper. Keep warm.

Garnishings:
20 pickling onions
10 g (0.25 oz) butter
100 g (3.5 oz) slab bacon, cut into strips
1 Tb parsley, finely chopped

Peel onions. Cook in salted water until tender. Drain. Heat butter in a skillet. Fry bacon until crisp. Add onions and parsley. Stir well. Keep warm.
Return meat to sauce. Reheat carefully.

1 bunch parsley

Place goulash in center of plate. Sprinkle with onions and bacon. Garnish with parsley. Arrange the dumplings on the plate or serve separately.

Marinating:
7 days
Preparation:
40 minutes
Cooking time:
1 hour 30 minutes
Yields 4 servings

ZÜRCHER KESSELFLEISCH
Cured Pork, Ham and Bacon on Cabbage Salad (Zurich)

500 g (1 lb) pork breast, pickled, cooked
250 g (8.75 oz) ham, cooked
200 g (7 oz) bacon, cooked
1.5 l (6⅓ cups) bouillon

Slice meats into serving pieces. In a saucepan heat bouillon. Add meat and slowly warm up.

Salad:
1 large white cabbage
Salt
20 g (0.75 oz) butter
1 onion, finely chopped
60 g (2 oz) bacon, cut into strips
1 dl (½ cup) beef stock
0.3 dl (⅛ cup) herb vinegar
0.6 dl (¼ cup) sunflower oil
Salt, freshly ground pepper

Clean, trim and quarter cabbage. Remove stalk. Wash thoroughly. Drain. Slice into fine strips. Fill a kettle with cold water. Add salt. Bring to the boil. Blanch cabbage for 1 minute. Drain well.
Heat butter in a skillet. Sauté onions. Add bacon and sauté. Blend onions, bacon, bouillon, vinegar and oil with cabbage. Season with salt and pepper.

Vinaigrette:
0.3 dl (⅛ cup) herb vinegar
1 dl (½ cup) safflower oil
1 Tsp chervil, finely chopped
1 Tsp parsley, finely chopped
1 twig thyme
1 pinch granulated sugar

In a bowl combine all ingredients for the vinaigrette.

Onion rings:
2 onions
2 Tbs sifted flour
Salt
3 dl (1¼ cups) cooking-oil

Peel onions. Slice into 3 mm (⅛ inch) rings. Dust with flour. Heat oil and fry onions until crisp and a golden brown. Drain on paper towel. Sprinkle with salt.

Place cabbage in center of plates. Set meats on top. Surround with vinaigrette. Garnish with fried onions.

Preparation:
20 minutes
Cooking time:
30 minutes
Yields 4 servings

AARGAUER RÜEBLITORTE
Carrot Cake with Vanilla Sauce and Café au Lait Ice-Cream

4 egg yolks
230 g (8.25 oz) granulated sugar
Grated rind of ½ lemon
220 g (7.75 oz) carrots
180 g (6.5 oz) almonds, finely ground
1 Tsp ground cinnamon
2 Tbs corn starch
2 big pinches baking powder
1 pinch salt
4 egg whites
Butter for the cake pan
Flour for dusting

Vanilla Sauce (s. p. 209)

Café au lait ice-cream:
2 dl (⅞ cup) whipping cream
2 dl (⅞ cup) milk
2 dl (⅞ cup) strong coffee
6 egg yolks
50 g (1.75 oz) granulated sugar

Confectioner's sugar
8 leaves fresh mint

In a bowl combine egg yolks, sugar and grated lemon rind. Beat until light and yellow-colored. Peel the carrots and grate finely. Stir into egg mixture. Add almonds, cinnamon and baking powder. Beat until smooth.
Preheat oven to 170°C (350°F).
Combine egg whites and salt in a mixing bowl. Beat until stiff. Carefully fold into cake mixture. Butter cake pan. Dust with flour. Turn the mixture into the cake pan. Place in the oven and bake for 50–60 minutes. Unmold cake and let cool.

In a saucepan combine cream, milk and coffee. Bring to a boil. In a bowl beat egg yolks and sugar until light and lemon-colored. Gradually beat the hot liquid into the egg mixture. Return to saucepan. Beat over low heat until cream thickens. Do not boil. Let cool and freeze.

Dust the cake with confectioner's sugar. Cut into 8 pieces and set on dessert plates. Surround with vanilla sauce and place 1 scoop of ice-cream beside the cake. Decorate with chopped mint leaves.

Preparation:
20 minutes
Cooking time:
1 hour 10 minutes
Yields 8 servings

142

ENGADINER NUSSTORTE
Engadine Nut-Cake with Stewed Plums

180 g (6.5 oz) butter
150 g (5.5 oz) sifted flour
350 g (12.25 oz) granulated sugar
2 eggs
1 pinch salt

Place the flour in a mixing bowl. Cut the butter into small pieces. Rub the flour and butter rapidly between the tips of your fingers. Add eggs, salt and sugar. Blend quickly into a smooth dough. Cool in the refrigerator for 1 hour.

Preparation:
1 hour 20 minutes
Cooking time:
1 hour 10 minutes
Yields 4 servings

130 g (4.5 oz) granulated sugar
100 g (3.5 oz) ground walnuts
150 g (5.25 oz) walnuts, coarsley chopped
2.5 dl (1 cup) whipping cream
1 Tb honey

In a small saucepan caramelize the sugar until a light-brown. Stir in all the nuts. Mix well. Add cream and honey. Bring to the boil. Let cool.
Preheat oven to 180°C (356°F).

Butter for the cake pan
Flour for dusting
2 Tbs red-currant jelly
1 egg yolk

Roll out ⅓ the dough to a thickness of 3 mm (⅛ inch). Butter a false-bottomed cake pan (26 cm [10¼ inches] in diameter). Dust with flour. Line the cake pan with the dough leaving a 3.5 cm (1⅜ inches) edge. Prick the dough with a fork. Spread the bottom with red-currant jelly. Pour the nut-mixture into the pan. Spread out evenly. Roll out remaining dough. Cut into a circle the size of the baking pan. Cover nut mixture. Press edges together. Baste top with egg yolk. Bake for 50–60 minutes. Let cool.

Plums:
16 ripe unblemished plums
100 g (3.5 oz) granulated sugar
1 dl (½ cup) red wine
¼ Tsp ground cinnamon

Wash, pit and quarter plums. In a saucepan caramelize sugar until a light-brown. Add the plums and turn well. Moisten with wine. Add the cinnamon. Cook until tender.

Confectioner's sugar

Dust dessert plates with confectioner's sugar. Cut the nut cake into small portions and place in center of plate. Decorate with stewed plums.

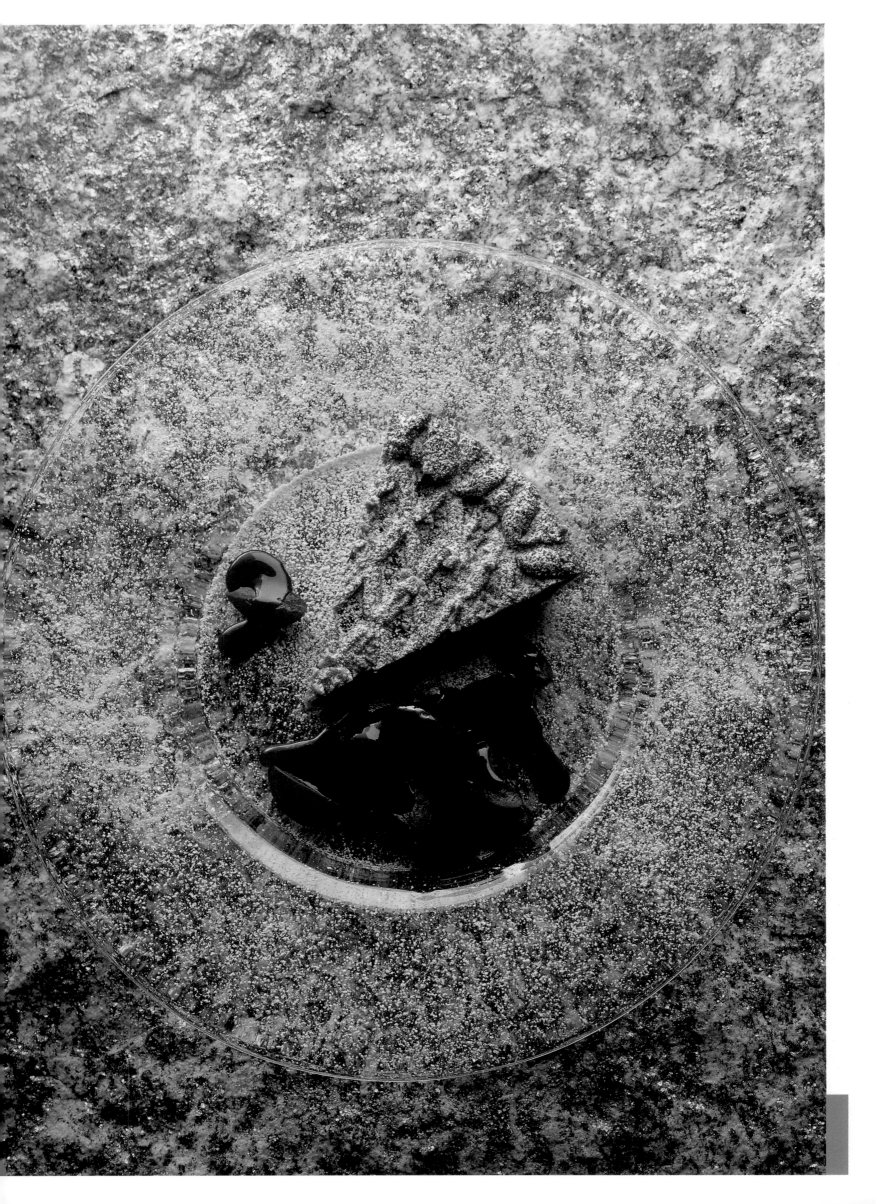

FRÜCHTEBROT
Fruit Bread

125 g (4.5 oz) butter
100 g (3.5 oz) granulated sugar
Grated rind of 1 lemon
4 eggs
100 g (3.5 oz) whole wheat flour
3 Tsp baking powder
125 g (4.5 oz) hazelnuts, finely ground
125 g (4.5 oz) slivered almonds
1 pinch cinnamon
1 pinch cardamom
70 g (2.5 oz) candied orange and lemon peel
150 g (5.25 oz) dried figs
125 g (4.5 oz) dried currants
50 g (1.75 oz) candied cherries

Preheat oven to 200°C (390°F).
In a mixing bowl beat butter and sugar until light and lemon-colored. Stir in eggs and grated lemon rind. Sift in flour and baking powder. Mix well. Add hazelnuts, almonds and spices. Chop candied fruits and figs. Add to mixture. Stir in currants. Work into a smooth dough.

Preparation:
30 minutes
Cooking time:
50–60 minutes
Yields 2 loaves

Butter for the cake pan

Butter a sheet of aluminium foil and line cake pan. Transfer batter to cake pan. Smooth out top with a spatula. Set pan in oven and bake for 50–60 minutes. Unmold cake and cool on a rack.
If the bread is for immediate consumption, remove the foil. For storage do not remove the foil.

Confectioner's sugar

To serve cut bread into slices 0.5 cm (³⁄₁₆ inch) thick. Dust with confectioner's sugar. Serve with tea, coffee or white wine.

If you prefer a light colored bread, substitute the ground hazelnuts with the same amount of skinned, ground almonds. The fruit bread can be stored in a metal box up to three weeks. The bread develops its full flavour after 2–3 days.

NUSSBROT
Nut Bread

4 dl (1¾ cups) milk
40 g (1.5 oz) compressed yeast
500 g (1 lb) all-purpose flour
160 g rye flour
35 g (1.25 oz) granulated sugar
15 g (0.5 oz) salt

In a small saucepan warm 1 dl (½ cup) milk. Add the yeast and dissolve. Place flour in a mixing bowl. Gradually mix in 2 dl (⅞ cup) milk and yeast mixture. Warm remaining milk. Dissolve sugar and salt. Add to the mixture.

100 g (3.5 oz) butter
200 g (7 oz) dried currants
300 g (10.5 oz) walnuts, quartered

Work butter, nuts and currants into dough. Knead thoroughly until smooth. Cover with a damp cloth and allow to rise for 30 minutes at room temperature. Preheat oven to 200°C (390°F).

1 egg
Butter for the baking sheet

Knead dough thouroughly. Divide into 2 portions and form loaves. Allow to rise for 15 minutes more. Beat egg and baste breads. Place on buttered baking sheet. Bake for 40 minutes. Cool on rack.
Nutbread is usually served with butter, jam and cheese.

Preparation:
1 hour
Cooking time:
40 minutes
Yields 2 loaves

ZÜRCHER ÖPFELBACHIS
Shredded Dough-Cake with Apples

4 Tbs walnuts
0.5 dl (¼ cup) milk

If the walnuts are fresh peel them. Quarter and soak in milk. Preheat oven to 220°C (428°F).

Preparation:
20 minutes
Cooking time:
15 minutes
Yields 4 servings

Batter:
80 g (2.75 oz) sifted flour
1.5 dl (⅔ cup) milk
1 dl (½ cup) whipping cream
40 g (1.5 oz) granulated sugar
½ vanilla bean, seeds scraped
Grated rind of ½ lemon
1 pinch salt
1 Tb kirsch
3 eggs

In a bowl combine flour, milk, cream, sugar, vanilla seeds, grated lemon rind, salt and kirsch. Beat into a smooth batter. Add the eggs and mix well.

Apples:
3 apples, tart variety
30 g (1 oz) sugar
20 g (0.75 oz) butter
30 g (1 oz) dried currants

Peel, core and quarter apples. Cut into 5 mm (³⁄₁₆ inch) wedges. In a saucepan caramelize the sugar until a light brown. Add apples and turn well. In a anti-adhesive skillet heat the butter and pour in the batter. Place the skillet in the oven. As soon as the batter has turned golden-brown and the surface has dried somewhat (about 5 minutes), shred the dough into small pieces. Drain the walnuts and add to dough. Stir in the apples and the currants. Mix well.

3 Tbs confectioner's sugar
1 Tsp ground cinnamon

Place on plates. Dust with confectioner's sugar and cinnamon.

ZWETSCHGENMOUSSE
Plum Mousse with Gingerbread Sauce

3 sheets gelatin
1 kg (2 lbs) ripe
unblemished plums
50 g (1.75 oz) granulated
sugar
1 dl (½ cup) red wine
¼ Tsp ground cinnamon
2 dl (⅞ cup) whipping
cream

Sauce:
0.5 dl (¼ cup) milk
1.5 dl (⅔ cup) whipping
cream
2 vanilla beans, slit open
lengthwise
2 Tbs gingerbread spices

3 egg yolks
40 g (1.5 oz) granulated
sugar
1 Tb plum brandy or kirsch

1 bunch fresh mint leaves
2 Tbs heavy cream
Confectioner's sugar
for decoration

Soak the gelatin in little water.
Wash and pit the plums. In a saucepan caramelize the sugar until a light brown. Moisten with wine. Add the plums and the cinnamon. Stir and cook until very tender. Purée in a blender and strain through a fine sieve. Drain the gelatin. Melt in small saucepan over moderate heat. Stir into plum purée. Beat cream until stiff. Fold into purée. Transfer mixture to a bowl. Cover and chill for at least 3 hours.

In a saucepan combine milk, cream, vanilla beans and gingerbread spices. Bring to the boil.

Beat egg yolks and sugar until light and lemon-colored. Over low heat gradually stir the hot liquid into egg mixture. Do not boil! Let cool. Stir in the brandy or kirsch.

Remove mousse from refrigerator. Form balls with a scoop or 2 tablespoons dipped in hot water. Place 2 on each plate. Surround with sauce and decorate with a few blobs heavy cream and draw them out with the back of a knife or a fork. Garnish with mint leaves and dust with confectioner's sugar.

Preparation:
30 minutes
Cooking time:
20 minutes
Yields 6 servings

BASLER MEHLSUPPE
Flour Soup (Basle)

2 onions

60 g (2 oz) lard or walnut oil
60 g (2 oz) sifted flour
5 dl (2⅛ cups) beef stock
6 dl (2½ cups) water

Salt, freshly ground pepper
Nutmeg
Marjoram
2 Tbs sour cream

Grated Sbrinz or Gruyère
Dark bread

Slice onions finely.

Heat lard or oil in a large saucepan. Add flour and with a wooden spatula stir continuously until flour turns brown. The flour should not turn lumpy. Add onions and sauté until light yellow. Cover with stock and water. Stir well. Cover pan with a lid and simmer for 2½ hours.

Purée soup in a blender. Strain through a fine sieve. Season with salt, pepper, nutmeg and marjoram. Stir in sour cream.

Transfer soup to a tureen. Serve with grated cheese and dark bread.

Preparation:
15 minutes
Cooking time:
3 hours
Yields 4 servings

BERNER ERBSENSUPPE
Pea Soup with Salted Pork Knuckles (Berne)

1 onion
30 g (1 oz) bacon rind
¼ leek
1 carrot
20 g (0.75 oz) butter
120 g (4.25 oz) split yellow peas
1.2 l (5 cups) bouillon

Chop onion finely. Dice bacon rind. Chop leek and carrot coarsely. Heat butter in a saucepan. Sauté onions and bacon rind. Add leeks and carrots. Sauté briefly. Stir in peas. Mix well. Cover with bouillon. Simmer for 1½ hours.

1.5 dl (⅔ cup) whipping cream
1 Tb fresh marjoram
Salt, freshly ground pepper

Purée soup in a blender. Rub through a fine sieve. Stir in cream. Bring to the boil. Chop marjoram finely and add to soup. Season with salt and pepper.

2 large potatoes

Peel potatoes and dice. Cook in lightly salted water until tender.

2 salted pork knuckles, cooked

Bone knuckles. Cut into small pieces.

½ leek

Trim, wash and slice leek. Steam «al dente».

Fresh marjoram

Reheat soup. Thin with bouillon if necessary. Pour into soup plates. Place meat and potatoes in soup. Sprinkle with leeks. Garnish with marjoram.

Preparation:
20 minutes
Cooking time:
1 hour 40 minutes
Yields 4 servings

GENFER SAIBLINGE
Char in Red Wine- and Onion Sauce with Spinach Flan (Geneva)

8 fillets of char, skinned
Salt, freshly ground
white pepper

Bone fish with a pair of tweezers. Season with salt and pepper. Fold over. Set aside.

Spinach flan:
300 g fresh spinach
1 dl (½ cup) whipping
cream
5 egg yolks
2 Tbs onions
1 pinch garlic
1 pinch nutmeg

Wash spinach. Remove stems. Chop onion finely. Mash garlic. Heat butter in a saucepan. Sauté onions and garlic. Add spinach and stir well. Moisten with cream. Bring to a boil. Season with salt and pepper. Purée in a blender and rub through a fine sieve. Stir in egg yolks and blend well.
Preheat oven to 150°C (302°F).
Line small ramekins with wax paper. Butter dishes and fill with flan mixture. Fill a roasting pan with boiling water. Line bottom with a newspaper. Set ramekins in pan. Poach flans in oven for 30 minutes.

Sauce:
2 onions
3 dl (1¼ cups) Pinot noir
10 g (0.25 oz) butter
0.5 dl (¼ cup) veal stock
(s. p. 207)
Salt, freshly ground pepper
80 g (2.75 oz) butter,
chilled

Chop onions finely. Heat butter in a small saucepan. Sauté onions. Moisten with wine. Cover with veal stock. Over low heat boil down to ¼ of its volume. Cut the butter into small cubes and whisk into sauce. Correct seasoning. Keep warm.

15 g (0.5 oz) butter

Heat butter in a large skillet. Place fish in pan and brown briefly on both sides. Remove from pan. Keep warm.

1 bunch chervil
1 twig dill

Carefully reheat the sauce. Unmold spinach flans and turn on upper part of serving plate. Remove wax paper. Spoon the sauce on lower part of plate and place the fish fillets diagonally into sauce. Garnish with chervil and dill.

Preparation:
20 minutes
Cooking time:
45 minutes
Yields 4 servings

ZÜRCHER SALAT-KOMPOSITION
Salad with Head Cheese, Veal Tongue and Fried Potatoes with Bacon (Zurich)

1 small onion
1 small carrot
50 g (1.75 oz) knob celery
1 cured veal tongue
about 350 g (13 oz)
400 g (14 oz) head cheese
1 bay leaf
1 clove
3 dl (1¼ cups) water
Salt

Clean, trim and dice vegetables. Pour the water into a kettle. Add salt. Place tongue, head cheese, vegetables and spices into pan. Bring to the boil. Reduce heat and simmer for 2 hours.

Preparation:
20 minutes
Cooking time:
2 hours 20 minutes
Yields 4 servings

Salad:
50 g (1.75 oz) watercress
50 g (1.75 oz) lambs lettuce
1 head chicory (endive)
100 g (3.5 oz) various
salad greens
1 bunch red radishes
8 cherry tomatoes
0.5 dl (¼ cup) vinegar
of Modena
1.5 dl (⅔ cup) safflower oil
or sunflower oil
Salt, freshly ground pepper

Clean, trim and wash salads. Drain well. Quarter cherry tomatoes. Slice radishes. Blend all ingredients for the vinaigrette.

300 g (1.5 oz) potatoes

Peel potatoes. Cut into small cubes. In a saucepan bring water to the boil. Add salt. Blanch potatoes for 1 minute. Drain.

50 g (1.75 oz) slab bacon
30 g (1 oz) butter
Salt

Dice bacon. Heat butter in a skillet. Add bacon and potatoes. Sauté until a golden brown.

Arrange salad on plates. Slice head cheese and tongue finely. Set on salad. Brush with vinaigrette. Decorate with tomatoes and radishes. Sprinkle with potatoes.

162

AMRISWILER BUURETOPF
Marinated Beef Knuckle with Dried Fruits and Vegetables

1 kg (2 lbs) beef knuckle, boned and cut into cubes 40 g (1.75 oz) each

Marinade:
3 dl (1¼ cups) red wine
3 dl (1¼ cups) water
3 shallots, coarsely chopped
120 g (4.25 oz) carrots, diced
80 g (2.75 oz) knob celery, diced
1 clove garlic, chopped
40 g (1.5 oz) parsley root, chopped
3 cloves
1 bay leaf
10 peppercorns
1 Tsp granulated sugar
1 Tsp salt

Soak dried fruits overnight.
Place meat in a bowl and combine with all ingredients for the marinade. Mix well. Cover bowl. Marinate in the refrigerator for 3 days.

Marinating:
3 days
Preparation:
15 minutes
Cooking time:
2 hours
Yields 4 servings

160 g (5.25 oz) dried fruits (pears, prunes, raisins, apples)
4 dl (1¾ cups) black tea
5 cloves
1 stick cinnamon
1 orange, rind
1 lemon, rind

One day ahead of time marinate fruits. Combine all ingredients in a bowl and cover.

2 Tbs cooking-oil
5 dl (2⅛ cups) red wine
2.5 dl (1 cup) marinade

Preheat oven to 180°C (356°F).
Remove meat from marinade. Dry with a clean cloth. Strain marinade through a fine sieve. Set marinade and vegetables aside separately.
In a fireproof casserole heat oil. Brown meat well on all sides. Add vegetables from marinade. Brown. Moisten with wine. Cover with marinade. Drain dried fruits. Add to meat. Cover casserole. Set in oven. Braise meat for 1½ hours.

2 dl (⅞ cups) whipping cream
Salt, freshly ground pepper

Remove meat and fruits from casserole. Keep warm. Remove spices from sauce. Stir in cream. Boil until sauce thickens. Return meat to sauce. Correct seasoning.

2 carrots
½ knob celery
½ cucumber
1 Tsp parsley, finely chopped
20 g (0.75 oz) butter

Clean and trim vegetables. Cut into slices. Cook «al dente» in lightly salted water. Drain. Heat butter and sauté vegetables briefly. Add parsley.

1 twig parsley

Arrange meat in center of plate. Decorate with vegetables. Garnish with parsley. As a side dish serve fried potatoes.

BERNER BAUERNGULASCH
Bernese Farmer's Stew (Berne)

400 g (14 oz) beef (neck)
200 g (7 oz) lamb (neck)
200 g (7 oz) bacon, diced

Cut meat into cubes about 30 g (1 oz) each. Or, have your butcher do it. Preheat oven to 180°C (356°F).

2 onions
1 leek
2 carrots

Chop onions finely. Clean trim and dice leeks and carrots.

2 Tbs cooking-oil
1 Tb tomato paste
2 Tbs sifted flour
1.2 l (5 cups) beef bouillon
Salt, freshly ground pepper

Season meat with salt and pepper. Heat oil in a fire-proof casserole. Brown meat well on all sides. Add vegetables and sauté briefly. Stir in tomato paste. Dust with flour. Turn well. Moisten with bouillon. Cover casserole. Set in oven and braise meat for 1½–2 hours.

400 g (14 oz) pickling onions
20 g (0.75 oz) butter
1 Tb granulated sugar
1 twig thyme
2 Tbs herb vinegar
1 dl (½ cup) beef bouillon

Peel pickling onions. Heat butter in a saucepan. Add onions. Sauté briefly. Sprinkle with sugar. Add thyme. Caramelize lightly. Moisten with vinegar. Cover with bouillon. Glaze for 10 minutes. Season with salt. Keep warm.

600 g (1¼ lbs) young round potatoes
1 Tb grape-seed oil
50 g (1.75 oz) butter
Salt
Thyme (optional)

Peel potatoes. Cook in lightly salted water for 5 minutes. Drain. Heat oil and butter in a skillet. Sauté potatoes until a golden brown. Season with salt. Sprinkle with thyme (optional). Keep warm.
Remove meat from casserole. Strain sauce through a fine sieve and return to casserole. If the sauce is very thin, boil down until it thickens somewhat. Correct seasoning. Return meat into sauce and reheat.

1 large twig parsley

Place stew in center of plates. Surround with potatoes and onions. Garnish with parsley.
As side dish serve green beans.

Preparation:
20 minutes
Cooking time:
2 hours 20 minutes
Yields 4 servings

GEBACKENE SIEDFLEISCHPLÄTZLI

Fried Slices of Pot-au-feu with Potato Dumplings

Potato dumplings:
750 g (1²/₃ lbs) potatoes
180 g (6.25 oz) sifted flour
1–1.5 dl (½–¾ cup) milk
30 g (1 oz) butter
1–2 egg yolks
Salt, freshly ground pepper
Nutmeg

Boil potatoes in their skin. Peel while still hot. Pass through the food mill. Mix with flour. Gradually stir in milk, butter and egg yolks. Work into a smooth dough. Season with salt and pepper. Roll the dough into strings of about 1–1½ cm (³/₈–⁹/₁₆ inches) in length. Cut into 2 cm (³/₁₆ inch) pieces, place on the palm of your hand and press with a fork. Fill a kettle with cold water. Salt and bring to the boil. Simmer the dumplings for 8–10 minutes. Remove and keep warm.

Pot-au-feu slices:
400 g (1 lb) boiled
pot-au-feu, in one piece
Salt
2 Tsp mustard
2 Tbs sifted flour
2 Tbs cooking-oil

Cut the pot-au-feu into thin slices. Season with salt. Spread with mustard on either side and dust with flour. Heat the oil and sauté meat well on both sides. Set aside and keep warm.

Sauce:
2 small shallots
20 g (0.75 oz) butter
2 dl (⁷/₈ cup) red wine
2 dl (⁷/₈ cup) veal stock
(s. p. 207)
1 Tsp mustard
30 g (1 oz) butter
Salt

Chop shallot finely. Heat butter and sauté shallots briefly. Moisten with wine. Cover with veal stock. Boil down to half its volume. Stir in mustard and butter. To make it light in texture pour sauce into a blender or use a hand-mixer. Correct seasoning. Keep warm.

20 g (0.75 oz) butter

Heat the butter in a skillet. Sauté dumplings until golden brown.

Place the dumplings on the upper part of the plate. Pour some sauce into the lower part. Place the meat on top of sauce.

Preparation:
25 minutes
Cooking time:
1 hour 20 minutes
Yields 4 servings

GESCHMORTE SCHWEINSHAXE
Braised Pig's Knuckles in Beer with Potato Gratin

1 onion
4 prunes
20 g (0.75 oz) butter
150 g (5.5 oz) uncooked
veal sausage meat
1 Tb chervil
Salt, freshly ground pepper
2 pig's knuckles, cured,
boned
2 Tbs cooking-oil
6 dl (2½ cups) dark beer
1 dl (½ cup) red wine
4 dl (1¾ cups) veal stock
(s. p. 207)
0.5 dl (¼ cup) whipping
cream
3 Tbs honey

Chop onion. Pit and quarter prunes. Chop chervil finely. Heat butter. Sauté onions until golden brown. Stir in prunes and chervil. Sauté briefly. Transfer to a mixing bowl. Add veal sausage meat. Mix well. Season with salt and pepper.
Preheat oven to 180°C (356°F).
Stuff knuckles with the mixture. Tie with string. Season. Heat oil in a large pan. Sear knuckles well on all sides. Moisten with beer and wine. Bring to a boil and cook until liquid has boiled down somewhat. Add the veal stock and cream. Bring back to the boil. Spoon honey over knuckles. Set pan in oven and braise for 2–2½ hours.

Preparation:
45 minutes
Cooking time:
2 hours 30 minutes
Yields 4 servings

Potato gratin:
500 g (1 lb) potatoes
4 dl (1¾ cups) whipping
cream
50 g Gruyère, grated
Salt, freshly ground pepper
Nutmeg
Butter for gratin dish

Peel potatoes and slice finely. Transfer to a bowl. Add cream and cheese. Season with salt, pepper and nutmeg. Stir well. Transfer potatoes to a buttered gratin dish. Cook in oven for 1½ hours.

Vegetables:
2 large zucchini
2 large potatoes
1 knob celery
10 g (0.25 oz) butter

Clean, wash and trim vegetables. Cut into sticks about 4 cm (1⁹⁄₁₆ inches) long. Cook in salted water until «al dente». Drain well. Heat butter and sauté vegetables. Set aside. Keep warm.

30 g (1 oz) butter

Remove knuckles from pan. Keep warm. Strain the sauce through a fine sieve into a small saucepan. Bring to a boil. Season with salt and pepper. Whisk in the butter.

Slice the knuckles and place on lower part of plates. Nap with sauce. Set potato gratin above. Sprinkle and surround with vegetables.

GROSSMÜETIS DÖRRBOHNEN
Grandma's Dried Beans, as a Side Dish with Smoked Spare-Ribs

250 g (8.75 oz) dried green beans
1.2 l (5 cups) water
1½ Tsp salt

120 g slab bacon
1 Tsp savory
2 onions
2 cloves garlic
1 Tb parsley
½ Tsp flour
2 dl (⅞ cup) beef stock
Salt, freshly ground pepper

Soak the beans one day in advance.
Drain beans. Bring water to the boil. Add salt. Boil beans for 30 minutes.

Dice bacon. Chop onions, savory and parsley finely. Mash garlic. Heat a skillet without adding grease and sauté the bacon well. Stir in onions, garlic and herbs. Dust with flour. Stir well. Moisten with beef stock. Drain beans and add to bouillon. Cook over moderate heat for 30 minutes. Season with salt and pepper.

Preparation:
20 minutes
Cooking time:
1 hour 15 minutes
Yields 4 servings

SOLOTHURNER LEBERPÄCKLI
Liver Paupiettes on Onion Purée with Butter-Wine Sauce and Fried Sage

80 g (3 oz) caul of pork

Onion Purée:
300 g (9.5 oz) onions
0.5 dl (¼ cup) milk
2 Tbs whipping cream
1 pinch ground nutmeg
1 pinch sugar
Salt, freshly ground
white pepper

Paupiettes:
4 slices slab bacon
4 slices calf's liver,
30 g (1 oz) each
4 sage leaves, finely
chopped
80 g (3 oz) crepinette
(caul) of pork (see above)
Salt, freshly ground pepper

Butter-Wine Sauce:
0.5 dl (¼ cup) veal stock
(s. p. 207)
3 dl (1¼ cups) Pinot noir
70 g (2.5 oz) butter

Fried Sage:
12 sage leaves
4 Tbs sifted flour
1 Tb dry white wine
Salt, freshly ground pepper
2 Tbs melted butter
Oil for frying

30 g clarified butter

1 Tb whipped cream

Sage blossoms or fresh
chervil for decoration

Soak the caul in cold water.

Peel onions and chop. Place in a saucepan. Add milk and cream. Season with salt and pepper. Bring to a boil. Cook until tender. Purée in a mixer and strain through a fine sieve. Return to saucepan and stir in whipped cream. Set aside and keep warm.

Sauté the bacon.
Drain caul well. Spraed out and cut 4 squares (10x15 cm [4x6 inches]). Place a slice of liver in the center of each square and cover with one slice of bacon. Sprinkle with sage and roll up. Season with salt and pepper. Wrap tightly in caul.

Combine wine and veal stock in a saucepan. Boil down until mixture reaches a syrup-like consistency. Whisk in the butter. Season with salt and pepper.

In a bowl combine flour, wine and melted butter. Beat into a smooth batter. Season with salt and pepper. Heat the oil for frying. Dip the sage leaves into the batter and fry until crisp.

In a skillet heat the clarified butter. Sear the paupiettes well on all sides. Reduce the heat and continue the cooking process for another 5–6 minutes.

Reheat the onion purée. Stir in 1 Tb whipped cream. Carefully reheat the sauce.

Place the onion purée in the center of the plates. Slice the paupiettes diagonally and set on top of the purée. Surround with sauce and decorate with fried sage. Garnish with sage blossoms or fresh chervil leaves.

Preparation:
20 minutes
Cooking time:
1 hour 20 minutes
Yields 4 servings

SPATZ ODER POT-AU-FEU
Pot-au-feu (Boiled Beef)

400 g (14 oz) beef
(brisket, rump, sirloin tip
or bottom round)

Cut meat into cubes about 40 g (1.5 oz) each.

Preparation:
20 minutes
Cooking time:
1 hour 15 minutes
Yields 4 servings

3 l (12½ cups) beef bouillon
100 g (3.5 oz) carrots
100 g (3.5 oz) leek
100 g (3.5 oz) knob celery
1 bunch parsley
1 bay leaves
3 cloves
Salt, freshly ground pepper
Nutmeg

Pour bouillon into a large kettle, salt and bring to a boil. Add the meat. Wrap the herbs and the spices in a piece of cheese cloth and tie. Add to bouillon. Let meat simmer for 60 minutes. Skim from time to time.
Remove meat from kettle. Keep in a warm place. Strain broth through a sieve into a smaller saucepan.

Garnishings:
4 baby carrots
4 baby leeks
4 baby turnips

Wash and trim the vegetables. Place in broth and cook until tender. Add the meat. Season with salt, pepper and nutmeg. Serve in soup plates.

SUURE MOCKE

Marinated Beef with Mashed Potatoes and Pattypan Squash

**800 g (1¾ lbs) beef
(London broil, flank)
120 g (4.25 oz) knob celery
2 cloves garlic
3 carrots
2 onions
½ leek
2l (8½ cups) red wine
2 bay leaves
2 cloves**

Place meat in a large bowl. Clean, trim and dice vegetables. Add to meat. Cover with wine. Add spices. Cover bowl and place in refrigerator for 1 week.

Marinating:
1 week
Preparation:
40 minutes
Cooking time:
2 hours 40 minutes
Yields 4 servings

**3 Tbs cooking-oil
2 Tbs tomato paste
3 dl (1¼ cups) beef stock
Salt, freshly ground pepper
40 g (1.5 oz) butter**

Preheat oven to 180°C (356°F).
Remove meat from marinade. Dry with a clean cloth. Save marinade. Heat oil in a fireproof casserole. Sauté meat well on all sides. Stir in tomato paste. Blend well. Moisten with marinade. Cover with beef stock. Place lid on casserole. Braise meat in oven for 2 hours. Remove meat from casserole. Keep warm. Strain sauce through a fine sieve into a small saucepan. Boil down to half its volume. Season with salt and pepper. Stir in butter.

**Potatoes:
1 kg (2 lbs) potatoes
Salt
2 dl (⅞ cup) milk
2 dl (⅞ cup) whipping
cream
50 g (1.75 oz) butter
Nutmeg**

Peel and quarter potatoes. Boil in lightly salted water until tender. Drain. Pass through the food mill. In a saucepan bring milk, cream and butter to the boil. Add potatoes. Blend well. Season with salt and nutmeg.

**Squash:
12 small pattypan squashes
20 g (0.75 oz) butter
1 twig thyme
1 dl (½ cup) vegetable
bouillon (s. p. 205)
Salt, freshly ground pepper**

Halve squashes crosswise. Heat butter in a large pan. Sauté squash. Add thyme. Moisten with bouillon. Season with salt and pepper. Cover and cook until tender.

Slice meat. Arrange meat, mashed potatoes and squash on plates. Spoon sauce over meat.

URNER HÄFELICHABIS
Goulash of Lamb, Goat, Beef and Pork with Cabbage

150 g (5.5 oz) lamb (shoulder)
150 g (5.5 oz) goat (shoulder)
150 g (5.5 oz) beef (shoulder)
Salt, freshly ground pepper
30 g (1 oz) cooking-oil

Trim meat and cut into cubes about 30 g (1 oz) each. Season with salt and pepper. Heat oil in a skillet. Sear meat well on all sides. Remove from pan. Keep warm.

1 white cabbage
2 onions
2 cloves garlic
10 g (0.25 oz) butter
5 dl (2⅛ cups) beef bouillon
1 clove
Salt, freshly ground pepper

Trim, clean and wash cabbage. Slice into fine strips. Chop onion. Mash garlic. In a saucepan heat butter. Sauté onions and garlic. Stir in cabbage and sauté briefly. Add meat and stir. Moisten with bouillon. Add clove. Cover and cook over low heat for 1½ hours.

500 g (1 lb) potatoes
Salt

Peel potatoes, quarter and cut off the edges. Boil until tender.

1 Tb chervil, finely chopped
40 g (1.5 oz) butter

Remove meat and cabbage from the saucepan. Set aside separately. Keep warm. Boil the bouillon down to 1 dl (½ cup). Whisk in the butter. Season with salt and pepper. Return cabbage to sauce and reheat.

Fresh chervil for garnishing

Place cabbage in the center of plates and set meat on top. Surround with potatoes. Garnish with chervil.

Preparation:
15 minutes
Cooking time:
2 hours
Yields 4 servings

WAADTLÄNDER KÄSEFONDUE
Cheese Fondue à la Vaudoise

300 g (10.5 oz) Gruyère cheese
200 g (10.5 oz) Emmental cheese
200 g (7 oz) Raclette cheese
200 g (3.5 oz) Fribourg Vacherin

Grate or shred the cheese.

1 glove garlic
4.5 dl (1⅞ cups) dry white wine

Peel the garlic. Halve. Rub the inside of a fondue dish (caquelon) with garlic. Pour the wine into the dish. Place dish on hot stove. Add the cheese and stir until it has melted.

3 Tbs corn starch
2 Tbs Kirsch
Freshly ground pepper
Nutmeg

Blend the corn starch with the kirsch. Stir into cheese. Bring back to a boil and stir continuously. Season with pepper and nutmeg. Transfer dish to burner and let simmer.

White bread
(preferably 2–3 days old)

Cut the bread into cubes.

Impale a piece of bread on the fondue fork and dip into the cheese.

Serve a dry white wine or black tea with a fondue. Top the meal with a small glass of kirsch.

Preparation:
15 minutes
Cooking time:
25–30 minutes
Yields 5–6 servings

BRÄNNTI SCHWYZER CRÈME
Crème Caramel with Almond Biscuits

Preparation:
25 minutes
Cooking time:
20 minutes
Yields 4–6 servings

Almond biscuits:
100 g (3.5 oz) slivered almonds
100 g (3.5 oz) granulated sugar
2 egg whites

Chop the almonds coarsely and blend with sugar. Beat egg whites lightly. Stir into almond mixture. Cover and keep in the refrigerator overnight.

Butter for the baking sheet
Empty mineral water bottles

Preheat oven to 200°C (390°F). Keep some clean mineral water bottles ready. Butter the backside of a baking sheet. Place 1 tablespoon of the almond mixture on the baking sheet. With the dome side of the spoon carefully spread the mixture outward into the shape of a thin, large circle. Leave a space of 2 cm (¾ inch) between the biscuits. Set baking sheet in the oven and bake biscuits for 8–10 minutes. With a spatula carefully remove biscuits and place over the side of the bottle. This procedure will give them the curved shape. Reduce the oven heat to 40°C (104°F) and place the bottles in the oven. Let the biscuits dry for 2 hours.

Crème brulée:
130 g (4.5 oz) granulated sugar
0.4 dl (¼ cup) dry white wine
3 dl (1¼ cups) whipping cream
2 dl (⅞ cup) heavy cream

In a small saucepan caramelize the sugar. Moisten with wine. Cover with cream. Bring to the boil.

50 g (1.75 oz) granulated sugar
2 egg yolks
0.5 dl (¼ cup) whipping cream

In a bowl beat egg yolks and sugar until light and lemon-colored. Gradually stir in the caramel/cream mixture. Return to pan. Beat vigorously over low heat until cream thickens. Do not boil! Strain through a fine sieve. Let cool and chill. Fold in the cream.

30 g (1 oz) granulated sugar

Caramelize sugar. Dip a wire-whisk into sugar mass. Move from left to right and draw caramel threads. Let dry.

Confectioner's sugar

Pour caramel cream into dessert plates. Decorate with caramel threads. Serve almond biscuits separately. Dust with confectioner's sugar.

BRISCHTNER NYTLÄ
Dried Pears Poached in Spiced Wine with Rice Pudding

3–4 dried pears per person
4 dl (1¾ cups) red wine
1 stick cinnamon
60 g (2 oz) granulated sugar
1 clove

Soak the pears one day in advance.
Drain the pears. In a small saucepan bring wine, cinnamon, sugar and clove to a boil. Add the pears and simmer for 20 minutes. Remove the pears. Set aside.

2 Tbs honey
1 Tb butter
½ lemon

Stir the honey into wine. Bring to a simmer. Reduce liquid over moderate heat to half its volume. Remove spices. Stir the butter into the sauce. Season with 2–3 drops of lemon juice. Keep warm.

Rice Pudding:
2 dl (⅞ cup) milk
50 g (1.75 oz) unpolished rice
Salt
1½ Tbs butter
Granulated sugar (optional)
Some freshly roasted walnuts
1 Tb kefir (or yogurt)
2 Tbs whipped cream

Bring milk to a boil. Add a pinch of salt. Stir in the rice and cook until tender. Stir the butter into the rice. Let cool.
Add some sugar (optional). Mix in the walnuts. Stir in the kefir and the whipped cream.

Angelica, finely chopped (for decoration)

Rice and pears should be served at room temperature. Arrange on dessert plates. Pour sauce around pears and rice-pudding. Garnish with chopped Angelica.

Preparation:
25 minutes
Cooking time:
45 minutes
Yields 4 servings

CARAMELISIERTER APFELKUCHEN
Caramelized Apple Tarts

110 g (4 oz) butter
40 g (1.5 oz) granulated sugar
1 egg
1 pinch salt
150 g (5.25 oz) sifted flour

Beat butter and sugar until light and lemon-colored. Beat egg and add to mixture. Stir in flour and salt. Rapidly work into a smooth dough. Chill for 30 minutes.

Preparation:
40 minutes
Cooking time:
20 minutes
Yields 4 small tarts

Butter for the flan rings
Flour

Preheat oven to 180°C (356°F).
Butter and flour flan rings 10 cm (4 inches) in diameter. Roll out a dough to a thickness of 2 mm (1⁄16 inch). Cut 4 circles about 12 cm (4¾ inches) in diameter. Line flan rings with dough. Prick with a fork.

Apples:
600 g (1¼ lbs) apples
30 g (1 oz) butter
30 g (1 oz) granulated sugar
½ vanilla bean, seeds
4 Tbs granulated sugar

Peel, core and quarter apples. Decorate the dome side with a few incisions to give it the look of a venetian blind. Arrange on flan rings.
Beat butter and sugar until light and lemon-colored. Add vanilla seeds. Blend well. Spread butter in flakes over apples. Sprinkle each tart with 1 Tb sugar. Bake for 20 minutes.

3 dl (1¼ cups) whipping cream
2 vanilla beans, seeds
2 Tbs confectioner's sugar

Beat cream until stiff. Stir in confectioner's sugar and vanilla seeds. Blend well. Chill.

Fresh mint leaves
Confectioner's sugar

Place tart in center of plate. With a spoon form walnut size cream balls. Set in center of tart. Garnish plate with mint leaves and dust with confectioner's sugar.

GLARNER ZIGERKRAPFEN
Curd Fritters with Plums and Gingerbread Ice-Cream (Glarus)

Ice-cream:
2 dl (⅞ cup) whipping cream
1 dl (½ cup) milk
1 vanilla bean, slit open
3 egg yolks
50 g (1.75 oz) granulated sugar
1 Tsp gingerbread spice

In a small saucepan combine cream, milk and vanilla bean. Bring to the boil. In a mixing bowl beat eggs and sugar until light and lemon-colored. Stir in gingerbread spice. Gradually stir hot liquid into egg mixture. Return to saucepan. Beat over low heat until custard thickens. Remove vanilla bean. Let cool. Freeze.

Fritters:
1 dl (½ cup) milk
1 pinch salt
30 g (1 oz) butter
250 g (8.75 oz) sifted flour

In a small saucepan heat milk to lukewarm. Add salt and butter. Turn in flour. Rapidly work into a smooth solid dough.

130 g (4.5 oz) curd
1 egg yolk
1 Tsp ground cinnamon
30 g (1 oz) dried currants
40 g (1.5 oz) hazelnuts, ground
Kirsch (optional)
1 egg white

In a mixing bowl combine all ingredients for the filling. Roll out the dough to a thickness of 2 mm (1/16 inch). Cut into circles (∅ 10–12 cm [4–5 inches]). Place 1 Tb filling in center of dough circles. Brush the edge with egg white. Fold into semicircles. Set aside.

Plums:
250 g (8.75 oz) firm ripe plums
50 g (1.75 oz) granulated sugar
0.5 dl (¼ cup) dry white wine
30 g (1 oz) walnut kernels, quartered
20 g (0.25 oz) dried currants
0.5 dl (¼ cup) plum brandy

Wash and pit the plums. Cut into eighths. In a small saucepan caramelize sugar. Add plums and turn well. Moisten with wine. Stir in walnuts, currants and brandy. Simmer until liquid reaches a syrup-like consistency. Set aside.

Sauce:
300 g (10.5 oz) plums
1 dl (½ cup) water
½ lemon, juice
80 g (2.75 oz) granulated sugar
0.5 dl (¼ cup) heavy cream
A dash of plum brandy (optional)

Wash and pit plums. In a saucepan combine plums, water, lemon juice, sugar and cream. Bring to the boil. Transfer to a blender and purée. Rub through a fine sieve. Add a dash of plum brandy (optional).

Oil for deep-frying

Heat oil. Deep-fry fritters until crisp. Drain on paper towel.

1 bunch fresh mint leaves

Coat plates with plum sauce. Set fritters in center. Place poached plums on one side and ice-cream on other side of fritters. Garnish with fresh mint leaves.

Preparation:
40 minutes
Cooking time:
30 minutes
Yields 4 servings

HONIG-APFELKUCHEN
Honey-Apple Cake with Vanilla Sauce

Pastry:
75 g (2.5 oz) butter
75 g (2.5 oz) honey
1 pinch nutmeg
1 pinch ground clove
1 pinch salt
1 Tsp ground cinnamon
150 g (5.25 oz) sifted flour
12 g (0.5 oz) baking powder

Beat the honey and the butter until smooth and fluffy. Stir in spices, flour and baking. Work into a smooth dough.
Preheat oven to 180°C (356°F).

800 g (1¾ lbs) apples, tart
Butter for the cake pan
Flour for dusting

Peel and core the apple. Cut into pieces of about 1x1 cm (⅜ inch). Work into pastry mixture and blend well. Butter a cake pan (28 cm [11 inches] long) and fill with cake mixture. Keep in a cool place for 30 minutes.

Glaze:
25 g (1 oz) honey
25 g (1 oz) butter
30 g (1 oz) coconut flakes
30 g (1 oz) walnuts

Beat honey and butter until creamy. Stir in the coconut flakes and the walnuts. Spread over top of the cake. Place cake pan in oven and bake for 50–60 minutes. Cover with aluminium foil if top browns too much. Unmold cake a cool on a rack.

Vanilla sauce (s. p. 209)

Decoration:
8 walnuts, halved
1 dl (½ cup) milk

The walnuts for garnishing have to be soaked in milk one day ahead of time. Dry well before use.

Fresh mint leaves

Cut the cake into slices. Place on dessert plates. Surround with vanilla sauce. Garnish with walnuts and mint leaves.

Preparation:
45 minutes
Cooking time:
1 hour
Yields 4 servings

OFEN-ÖPFEL
Grandma's Baked Apples with Vanilla Sauce

30 g (1 oz) almonds, ground
20 g (0.75 oz) hazelnuts, ground
Juice and grated rind of ½ lemon
0.5 dl (¼ cup) whipping cream
30 g (1 oz) raisins
1 Tb honey
30 g (1 oz) granulated sugar
20 g (0.75 oz) butter
1 Tb lingonberry or cranberry preserve

In a mixing bowl blend all ingredients for the stuffing. Preheat oven to 180°C (356°F).

Preparation: 20 minutes
Cooking time: 35 minutes
Yields 4 servings

4 medium-sized apples
1 lemon

Peel apples without removing stems. Cut a thin slice off the bottom of each apple. Cut ¼ from top. Core bottom part carefully. Place in a bowl of water. Add a few drops lemon juice.

Butter for the gratin dish
2 dl (⅞ cup) apple cider (or white wine)
50 g (1.75 oz) granulated sugar
30 g (1 oz) butter

Butter gratin dish. In a small saucepan bring cider or white wine and sugar to the boil. Transfer to gratin dish.
Stuff apples. Cover with tops. Set in gratin dish. Sprinkle with butter flakes. Bake for 35 minutes.

Vanilla Sauce (s. p. 209)

1 bunch lemon balm
2 Tbs black and white chocolate slivers

With a knive shave slivers off the chocolate bars. Coat plates with vanilla sauce. Place apple in center. Garnish with chocolate slivers and lemon balm.

SCHLAATEMER RICKLI
Plaited Loaves with Vanilla Sauce

3 eggs
130 g (4.5 oz) granulated sugar
1 pinch salt
Grated rind of ½ lemon
1 Tb kirsch
100 g (3.5 oz) melted butter
380 g (13.5 oz) sifted flour
1 Tsp baking powder

Vanilla Sauce (s. p. 209)

Oil for deep-frying

Garnishings:
30 g (1 oz) dark chocolate
1 Tb whipping cream
1 bunch fresh lemon balm
Confectioner's sugar

In a bowl combine eggs, sugar and salt. Beat until light and lemon-colored. Stir in the butter, kirsch and grated lemon rind. Add flour and baking powder. Knead into a smooth dough. Cover and cool for 30 minutes.

Plait the dough into small loaves about 10 cm (4 inches) long. Heat the oil and deep-fry until golden brown. Drain well.

In a small saucepan melt the chocolate. Stir in the cream. Place the loaves in the center of plates. Surround with vanilla sauce. Decorate with melted chocolate. Garnish with lemon balm and dust with confectioner's sugar.

Preparation:
45 minutes
Cooking time:
10 minutes
Yields 4 servings

SCHOKOLADENTERRINE
Chocolate Terrine with Vanilla- and Raspberry Sauce

Pralin:
30 g (1 oz) granulated sugar
30 g (1 oz) ground hazelnuts

Prepare the terrine one day ahead.
Caramelize the sugar in a small saucepan until it turns a light brown. Stir in the ground hazelnuts. Rinse a stainless steel or marble surface with cold water. Place the pralin immediately on the surface and let cool. Chop finely.

Preparation:
20 minutes
Cooking time:
20 minutes
Yields 6–8 servings

Terrine:
2.5 dl (1 cup) milk
100 g (3 oz) cooking chocolate
20 g (0.75 oz) semi-sweet chocolate
5 sheets gelatin
4 egg yolks
60 g (2 oz) granulated sugar
2 dl (⁷/₈ cup) whipping cream

Bring the milk to a boil. Add the chocolate and let melt. Soak the gelatin in little water. Beat the egg yolks and the sugar until fluffy and lemon-colored. Gradually beat the chocolate-milk into the egg mixture. Drain gelatin. Melt over low heat and add to the custard. Stir well. Place bowl in the refrigerator. Whip the cream. As soon as the custard starts to set stir in half of the chopped pralin and fold in the whipped cream. Transfer to a terrine and chill for 3–4 hours.

Vanilla Sauce (s. p. 209)

Raspberry Sauce:
100 g (3 oz) raspberries
0.5 dl (¼ cup) water
1 Tb confectioner's sugar
2 Tbs kirsch

Place the raspberries in a blender. Add the water. Purée and strain through a fine sieve. Stir in the confectioner's sugar and the kirsch.

Leaves of lemon balm

Unmold the terrine. Dip a knife into hot water and slice. Pour some vanilla cream on each plate and decorate with the raspberry sauce. Place a slice of the terrine in the middle of the plate. Sprinkle with the remaining pralin and garnish with fresh leaves of lemon balm.

Personal Notes

Personal Notes

VEGETABLE BOUILLON

2 carrots
1 leek
1 small knob celery
½ savoy cabbage
1 tomato
0.5 dl (¼ cup) olive oil
3 l (12 cups) water

Clean, trim and dice vegetables. Quarter tomato. Heat oil in a large saucepan. Sauté vegetables briefly. Cover with water. Bring to a boil.

Preparation:
15 minutes
Cooking time:
1 hour 40 minutes

2 onions
3 peppercorns, crushed
2 cloves
2 bay leaves
1 bunch parsley

Halve the onions. Do not peel. Heat stove. Place onion, dome side up, on the hot plate and brown. Add to bouillon. Simmer bouillon for 1½ hours. Strain through a fine sieve. Cool and chill. Freeze in small portions.

FISH STOCK

2 shallots
1 small leek
½ knob celery
1 carrot

1.5 kg (3.5 lbs) fresh fish,
fish heads and trimmings
0.5 dl (¼ cup) olive oil
2 dl (⅞ cup) dry white wine
4 l (4½ quarts) water
1 sprig dill
1 bay leaf
5 peppercorns, crushed

Clean, peel and trim the shallots and vegetables and cut into small pieces.

Wash the fish and trimmings under running cold water. Heat the oil and sauté the vegetables. Add the fish and trimmings. Cover with white wine. Add the water and bring to a boil. Skim and add the dill and spices. Simmer for 30 minutes. Strain through a clean cloth and let cool.

Stock should be prepared just before need arises. Or, freeze in small portions.

Preparation:
15 minutes
Cooking time:
30 minutes

VEAL STOCK

2 kg (4 lbs) cracked veal bones
2 Tb cooking-oil

½ knob celery
1 onion
2 carrots
1 tomato
½ leek

½ bottle red wine
2 l (8 cups) water
1 bay leaf
1 clove
4 black peppercorns

Preheat oven to 200°C (390°F).
Heat a large roasting pan. Add the oil and the bones. Brown for 2 hours. Stir a few times.

Clean, peel and trim the vegetables. Cut into small pieces. As soon as the bones have browned add the vegetables and roast together with the bones. Transfer bones and vegetables to a large kettle.

Moisten with the wine and transfer to kettle. Scrape up the juices with a little water and join with the bones. Cover with the water. Bring to a boil. Skim. Add the seasonings and simmer for 4 hours. Strain through a fine sieve or a clean cloth. Return to a saucepan and boil down to 2 dl (⅞ cup) liquid.

Freeze in small portions.

Preparation:
15 minutes
Cooking time:
6 hours

GAME STOCK

3 kg (6½ lbs) game bones
0.5 dl (¼ cup) cooking-oil

Preheat oven to 200°C (390°F).
Place bones in a roasting pan. Sprinkle with oil. Brown in the oven for 2 hours.

1 onion
1 large carrot
½ leek
100 g (3.5 oz) knob celery
5 dl (2⅛ cups) red wine

Halve the onion. Do not peel. Clean, peel and trim the vegetables. Dice. Add to the bones and brown for 1 hour. Moisten with the wine. Scrape up the juices.

4 l (4½ qts) water
4 juniper berries
1 sprig rosemary
1 sprig pine

Transfer to a large kettle. Add the water and the seasonings. Simmer for 2 hours. Strain through a sieve. Return liquid to a saucepan. Over low heat boil stock down by two thirds.

Let cool. Freeze in small portions.

Preparation:
15 minutes
Cooking time:
approx. 5 hours
Yields about
1 l (4 cups)

VANILLESAUCE

2 dl (⅞ cup) milk
2 dl (⅞ cup) whipping
cream
2 vanilla beans

4 egg yolks
60 g granulated sugar

Pour the milk and the cream into a small saucepan. Halve the vanilla beans lengthwise. Scrape out the seeds. Add beans and seeds to the liquid. Bring to a boil.

Beat the egg yolks and the sugar until fluffy and lemon-colored. Gradually beat the boiling liquid into the egg mixture and pour back into the saucepan. Set over moderate heat and beat with a wire whisk until custard reaches a smooth and creamy consistency. Do not boil!

Cool and chill.

Preparation:
10 minutes
Cooking time:
15 minutes
Yields about
5 dl (2⅛ cups)

Personal Notes

Personal Notes

Personal Notes